T0272681

This is vintage Wright. Based on a lifetime of theological reflection on Paul and his world, Tom Wright gives us a vigorous and exhilarating exposition of the Acts of the Apostles. Wright brings out not only the key points of the story of Acts but also (and more importantly) the theological ideas embodied in the story. In this "brief but not shallow" bird's-eye view of Acts, Wright invites us to journey with Paul and the other apostles as they set out on the adventure of witnessing to the risen Jesus in the sophisticated cultures of the Greek and Roman worlds — and at the same time to reflect on the challenges faced by followers of Christ today.

LOVEDAY ALEXANDER, professor emerita of
biblical studies, University of Sheffield

N. T. Wright's *The Challenge of Acts* is neither a light devotional nor a dense scholarly tome, but an easy-to-read summary of the Acts of the Apostles. Wright doesn't scrutinize every fact, but like a good tour guide in Jerusalem, Ephesus, or Corinth, he takes us to the biggest highlights, shows us some artifacts that most might miss, and ably explains why it should matter to us today. A great way to read the story about the beginnings of the early church.

REV. DR. MICHAEL F. BIRD, deputy principal,
Ridley College, Melbourne, Australia, coauthor,
The New Testament in Its World

Tom Wright describes Acts as "a page-turner." The same could be said for Wright's interpretive reflections on Acts, as he explores its twists of plot and overarching themes. From insightful analysis to thoughtful contextualization, *The Challenge of Acts* invites readers into a fresh encounter with this fascinating narrative of the earliest days of the church. Readers of all kinds, whether seasoned or new to the Bible, will benefit from this engaging study.

JEANNINE K. BROWN, The David Price Professor
of Biblical and Theological Foundations,
Bethel Seminary, Saint Paul, Minnesota

This little book is a retelling of the story of the New Testament book of Acts with the Wright spin. Unsurprisingly, this retelling is accomplished in the light of Wright's other extensive work in New Testament studies and research into Second Temple Judaism. For readers so inclined, footnotes point to Wright's fuller explanations in his other publications. Of course, readers who disagree with some of Wright's conclusions in other realms might chafe a bit at seeing how those ideas are brought over into his reading of Acts. But one must nevertheless appreciate Wright's willingness to sketch out the ramifications of his reading of Paul (for instance) on his reading of Luke. Thus, with this brief survey of Acts, Wright continues his attempt to demonstrate that the New Testament is better understood in light of its own first-century historical situation than it is when filtered through a Reformation grid from the sixteenth century. This might be a blinding glimpse of the obvious for some, but Wright's persistence in making and extending this argument will be seen as helpful—if not also necessary—for many.

Following Luke's lead, Wright regularly makes connections with the Old Testament. What God had announced in the Scriptures of Israel, Luke acknowledges in Acts as having reached a climactic turning point in the complex of the first-century Jesus-and-Spirit event. Much of what Wright says is familiar, and yet his connections of familiar with familiar have their own enlightening aha moments. At times Wright can subtly state the obvious, and at other times he obviously states the more subtle. Sometimes what the reader might have wanted Luke to mean in a favored section of Acts becomes less important because Wright takes Luke's nuanced way of saying things and clarifies that Luke intends something totally other than what has been produced by our preferential and oftentimes too narrow and atomized efforts at interpretation. *The Challenge of Acts* is an informative read.

> **DOUGLAS S. HUFFMAN,** professor of New Testament and dean of academic programs, Talbot School of Theology at Biola University, author of *The Story of Jesus Continues: A Survey of the Acts of the Apostles*

As always, Wright presents his insights in a highly readable, engaging, and often witty way, developing pervasive themes in Acts. Challenging many points of secular philosophies and popular fads along the way, he articulates a coherent theological picture that also challenges our hearts and lives in today's world.

CRAIG S. KEENER, F. M. and Ada Thompson Professor
of Biblical Studies, Asbury Theological Seminary,
author of *Acts: An Exegetical Commentary* (4 vols.)

Wright's very readable overview of Acts reflects the breathless wonder and challenge of Luke's account of the early spread of the good news that the risen and ascended Jesus now reigns as God's appointed king. This brief and accessible commentary not only charts a clear course through the twists and turns of Luke's action-packed narrative but also offers numerous insights into the practical and theological relevance of Acts for Christians today.

DAVID M. MOFFITT, reader in New Testament
Studies, University of St. Andrews

N. T. Wright's lectures on the Book of Acts are a deeply informed study for the general reader that deepens our understanding of Luke's historical record of the first thirty years of the proclamation, worship, theology, and missionary work of the earliest followers of Jesus Messiah. Anyone who thinks that studying historical events is a dry, deadening exercise that is best avoided will be forced to think again as Wright demonstrates the significance of Luke's second part of his long historical monograph on Jesus and his followers for Christian faith, and, not the least, for an increasingly secular world. Wright's newest book is a welcome study guide that deserves to be used widely.

ECKHARD J. SCHNABEL, Mary F. Rockefeller
Emeritus Distinguished Professor of New
Testament, Gordon-Conwell Theological
Seminary, author of *Acts* in the Zondervan
Exegetical Commentary on the New Testament

In this short yet substantive commentary, Tom Wright skillfully guides readers through the expansive and exciting Acts of the Apostles. Wright highlights several leading themes that animate Acts. He also helpfully focuses on the progress of the gospel as it advances—obstacles and opposition notwithstanding—from the Holy City to the Capital City by the power of the Holy Spirit and through the courageous witness of those who would come to be called "Christians." Acts challenges us, as does *The Challenge of Acts*, to an uncommon devotion to the Lord of heaven and earth, who is no less Lord of the church.

> **TODD D. STILL,** Charles J. and Eleanor McLerran DeLancey Dean & William M. Hinson Professor of Christian Scriptures, Baylor University, Truett Seminary, coauthor of *Thinking through Paul: A Survey of His Life, Letters, and Theology*

Tom Wright here gives us a good, accessible study of Acts that will help lots of people to engage with Acts better and with greater understanding. His "big picture" approach to the overall story of Acts is illuminating, beautifully written, and rooted in good scholarship. It will inform and help church members and those who preach and teach from Acts. Read it—you will benefit.

> **STEVE WALTON,** senior research fellow in New Testament, Trinity College, Bristol, author of *Acts 1–9:42* in the Word Biblical Commentary series

THE
CHALLENGE
OF
ACTS

*Rediscovering
What the Church
Was and Is*

N. T. WRIGHT

ZONDERVAN ACADEMIC

The Challenge of Acts

Published in Grand Rapids, Michigan, by Zondervan. Zondervan is a registered trademark of The Zondervan Corporation, L.L.C., a wholly owned subsidiary of HarperCollins Christian Publishing, Inc.

Requests for information should be addressed to customercare@harpercollins.com.

Also published in Great Britain in 2024

SPCK
SPCK Group
Studio 101
The Record Hall
16–16A Baldwin's Gardens
London EC1N 7RJ
www.spckpublishing.co.uk

ISBN 978-0-310-16799-0 (hardcover)
ISBN 978-0-310-16804-1 (audio)
ISBN 978-0-310-16803-4 (ebook)

Cover design: LUCAS Art & Design, Jenison, MI
Cover photo: © Turnervisual / Getty Images

Printed in the United States of America

24 25 26 27 28 LBC 6 5 4 3 2

For Jesse Chevallier Wright

Contents

N. T. Wright is research professor emeritus of New Testament and early Christianity at the University of St Andrews and senior research Fellow at Wycliffe Hall, Oxford. He is the author of more than eighty influential books, including *The New Testament for Everyone, Simply Christian, Surprised by Hope, The Day the Revolution Began, Paul: A Biography, Jesus and the Powers* (with Michael F. Bird) and *Into the Heart of Romans*.

Preface

This book offers a kind of bird's-eye view of the Acts of the Apostles. There is a lot to be said for verse-by-verse exegesis and exposition of the New Testament, but there is also a lot to be said for, on occasion, standing back and seeing the larger sweep of thought and noting the way certain themes are highlighted and developed. This is the latter sort of book. It takes Acts in four-chapter sequences, apart from the introduction and, as I explain below, the fuller treatment of Acts 17. Apart from a few references, I have not attempted to engage in any detail with contemporary scholarship, though people who know the field will see where I am making particular decisions. I often agree and sometimes disagree with other scholars, though without making that explicit. I have appended a list of resources for further study for any who want to follow things up.

The work began as a course of lectures given at Wycliffe Hall, Oxford, in the spring of 2023, and I was then able to develop and extend it further as the guest of South Main Baptist Church, Houston, Texas, in June of that year. I have kept some elements of the spoken style, though I have adjusted them throughout into a more 'written' mode.

My host for the lectures in Houston was South Main's Senior Pastor, Steve Wells, and I had the further sponsorship of Truett Seminary, under the leadership of Professor Todd D. Still. The whole event was co-ordinated by the team from N. T. Wright Online, now known as *Admirato*, under the leadership of Dr David Seemuth. So many people contributed to the smooth running of the event – this included arranging emergency dental treatment for me for a sudden infection that was threatening to make speaking painful. I am deeply grateful to them all.

When framing the Houston lectures, I had already decided to be led by the text into treating Paul's address in Athens in a particular way, devoting a whole lecture to that passage rather than simply continuing the method of treating four chapters at a time. While I was in Houston, I was invited by Mark Lanier to lecture as part of a conference at the Lanier Library, and I decided to develop the same themes further. I have allowed this fuller discussion to find its way into the treatment here, so that the chapter devoted to Acts 17 is somewhat longer, and applied in more detail to contemporary issues, than is the case in the rest of the book.

One particular note about usage: I have moved towards saying 'Judean' rather than 'Jew' or 'Jewish'. This enables us, I believe, to think historically about the way the ancient world saw the Judean Diaspora, rather than subtly importing particular modern meanings of 'Jew' or 'Jewish'.

Unless otherwise marked, quotations from the New Testament are taken or adapted from *The New Testament for Everyone*, third revised edition (London: SPCK; Grand Rapids, MI: Zondervan, 2023), abbreviated as *NTE*.

I am grateful, as ever, to Philip Law and his team at SPCK in London, and to Katya Covrett and her colleagues at Zondervan, for their help in bringing this book to completion. I am particularly grateful to Professor Steve Walton for his careful reading of an earlier draft and many helpful comments, though any errors that remain, whether of fact or judgement, are of course mine alone.

I am delighted to dedicate this book to my newest grandson, Jesse Chevallier Wright.

Tom Wright
Wycliffe Hall, Oxford

1

Acts 1

To the Ends of the Earth!

Introduction

This book offers a brief, though not shallow, introduction to the Acts of the Apostles. Acts is a substantial book, sitting there right in the middle of the New Testament, looking back to the four Gospels and on to the mission of the early church. It provides a framework for our understanding of the letters, but it also does more than that. It offers a sophisticated and nuanced view of what it meant to think of the gospel of Jesus, Israel's Messiah, going out into the world over which Israel's Messiah claims the status of lord. This meant confronting the wider culture of the Greek and Roman world, as well of course as the culture of the Judean world, within which the idea of messiahship itself meant what it meant – even when redefined around the crucified and risen Jesus. All of this is showcased in Acts, providing much food for thought as we ourselves face new questions about gospel and culture in our own confusing world.

Acts is a page-turner. Thirty years or more of early church history flash before our eyes: full of interest, lessons to be learned, characters to ponder. It's easy to cherry-pick parts that seem to speak to us directly; the danger then is that we miss themes that emerge in a more overarching way. Some of those are powerfully relevant to the challenging life and work to which the followers of Jesus are called today.

In this first chapter, I will focus on Acts 1 as an introduction to the whole book. Thereafter we will take four chapters at a time, focusing on particular passages. Thus in chapter 2, we will look at Acts 1 – 4 as a whole, proceeding thereafter in fours, and finally getting Paul to Rome in chapter 9 – having added a whole extra chapter to deal with the dense but vital and fascinating address of Paul in Athens (Acts 17). The division of chapters in Acts is mostly arbitrary. As is well known, the New Testament wasn't divided into 'chapters' and 'verses' until some centuries later. But it works well enough.

The one non-arbitrary division is that Acts itself naturally divides at the end of chapter 12. This corresponds to Jesus' commission to the disciples in 1:8: they are to bear witness to him in Jerusalem, Judea and Samaria – that's the first twelve chapters – and then 'to the very ends of the earth', which is chapters 13 – 28. Since all roads lead *to* Rome, all roads also led *from* Rome. Once the message was there, it would go out in all directions. Indeed, the idea of the 'message', the 'word', doing its own work – which is obviously a way of speaking of God himself being at work *through* the 'word' – is itself a major theme in Acts.[1] And, as we shall see, many first-century hearers of chapter 1 would already recognise in the claims of Jesus a clear, if implicit, challenge to those of Caesar.

The risen Jesus and the kingdom of God

So we begin at the beginning. Luke follows the frequent ancient custom of addressing his work to a named individual, who may be a patron, or simply a friend; or the name may even be a generic label for any well-intentioned reader – since *Theophilus* might mean 'God-lover'. This dedication matches the one at the start of Luke's Gospel, 'the previous book' as he says. There he had set out what Jesus had done and taught. As the disciples said on the Emmaus Road, Jesus was a prophet mighty in deed and word. But the crucial thing here, which determines how Luke wants us to read the whole

---

1 We might compare the various Old Testament passages in which 'the word' is the creative agent of the one God: e.g. Isaiah 40:8; 55:11. In Genesis 1, God speaks and the world is brought into being (compare too e.g. Psalm 33:6, 9).

book, is that he now speaks of all that Jesus *began* to do and to teach. In other words, the 'doing' and 'teaching' didn't stop.

How does this work out? Many times in Acts, we are told that the lord spoke to someone – often Paul – or stood by them on a particular occasion. But Jesus' involvement isn't limited to those explicit moments. Jesus is now not simply a figure either of the historical past or of the theological, heavenly present (though he is both of those as well). He is alive, active, directing, speaking, performing deeds of power. His work of instructing the disciples continued, as in verse 2, even in that strange period between Easter and Ascension. We should note, right there, that Luke tells us that Jesus gave them instruction *through the holy spirit* – in other words, though the spirit is poured out upon them in a new way in chapter 2, the spirit was already active, opening their minds and hearts.[2]

Verse 3 tells us the ground upon which the rest of the book will stand: the resurrection and the kingdom of God. Luke insists, of course, on the fact that after his death Jesus was found to be bodily alive. Everything in this book hinges on Jesus' resurrection, not simply as an odd dramatic miracle that God did for Jesus, but as the launching of God's new creation in the person of his son. Luke speaks here of Jesus offering 'proofs'. This implies that, already by the time he was writing, people had challenged the basic message about the Easter event and that Luke, like the others, had regularly referred them back to what had actually happened in those forty days.

Jesus' resurrection then becomes, of course, the key point in the confrontation with the wider world. This is so whether it's the Temple-hierarchy at the start of chapter 4 (who are annoyed because the disciples are announcing that the long-awaited resurrection has happened in the case of Jesus) or the high court at Athens in chapter 17, who mock Paul when he tells them that Jesus has been raised from the dead and will come again as judge. If the

---

2 I use lower case for 'spirit' because the early Christians used *pneuma* with no means of differentiating their particular referent from the many other meanings and referents which the word had in the philosophies of the day. Their usage had to make its own way in the world, as they themselves had to do.

message of the resurrection had simply been (as some in our own day would have it) that 'Jesus' cause continues' or that Jesus was alive in some 'spiritual' way (whatever that might have meant) but without anything happening to his body, nobody would have been shocked. But they were.

Anyway, the teaching of the risen lord in the short period before the ascension was focused on 'the kingdom of God'. Since that had been the central theme of Jesus' public career, it might come as a surprise that it isn't referred to very often in Acts. We have two references here, in verses 3 and 6; two references right at the end of the book, in 28:23 and 31; and just four other references in the whole of the rest of the book, each time functioning as a shorthand for 'what the apostles were generally talking about'. Not much, we might think, to be going on.

But this doesn't mean that Luke is playing it down. As in Paul's letters, the *phrase* 'kingdom of God' is largely absent because the *reality* – of Jesus as the sovereign lord, ruling over God's world – is everywhere present. So Acts has, as its two bookends, first the present passage with Jesus explaining about the kingdom, and then in chapter 28 Paul in Rome speaking 'openly and unhindered' (v. 31, RSV) about God as king and Jesus as lord. That tells you what the rest of the story is all about.

The phrase 'kingdom of God', after all, was already a shorthand, a slogan, in the Judean world of Jesus' day. It picked up on the celebration in the Psalms, and in Isaiah 52, of the promise that YHWH would come back to his world, back to Israel, would come back to rule and reign and sort everything out.[3] What Acts is going to tell us is what it looked like when that had happened: how that long hope was being implemented.

In verses 4–5, the disciples find themselves poised between John's baptism and the new spirit-baptism they are promised, which we meet in the next chapter. (This is one of those strange passages that appear to clash with the picture in Matthew and Mark, where the disciples meet Jesus on a mountain in Galilee; for Luke, all the

---

3 See e.g. Psalms 93:1; 97:1; 99:1; Isaiah 52:7.

meetings take place in or around Jerusalem. John, meanwhile, gives us both: some meetings in Jerusalem, some in Galilee. That untidiness, as many have pointed out, is one reason for supposing that the resurrection stories were not made up, and tidied up, a generation later. I've written about that elsewhere.[4])

More important, perhaps, is to reflect for a moment on John's baptism as the prelude to the spirit-baptism which is to follow. What, after all, was John doing? His work was reactivating the symbols of Israel's founding story, the exodus. He was saying, in effect, 'This is the time for the new exodus, and this is how you can be part of it!' In other words, it was an acted parable of the long-awaited redemption, the rescue of Israel from slavery to the dark powers of paganism, and the start of the journey to the promised inheritance. But, as in Paul (for instance, in Romans 8), the 'inheritance' is not, as most modern Christians might suppose, 'heaven'. The inheritance is God's promise to Abraham, amplified in his promises to David, concerning the whole world.[5] And, as in the original exodus, the way to the promised land was through God himself coming to dwell in the midst (Exodus 40), to lead them there. That is precisely what is now going to happen in the next chapter, with the gift of the spirit.

Kingdom and witness

This brings us to the disciples' key question in verse 6: 'Is this the time when you are going to restore the kingdom to Israel?' This question emerges, naturally enough, from considerable confusion. Jesus' friends had not of course been expecting his crucifixion and resurrection. Those shocking and tumultuous events were quite outside their sense of how God's great purposes would unfold. But the reason they had followed Jesus was because they had come to believe that he was Israel's Messiah, the king who would rescue

4 See my *RSG*, ch. 13. Abbreviations for my published works are listed in the suggestions for further reading.

5 See Romans 4:13; 8:12–30. Paul here looks back to e.g. Genesis 12:3; Psalm 2:8.

Israel and restore her fortunes at last. So, they are saying, 'Can we get all that back on track now? Is this the time to do what we had all along expected, what Deuteronomy and the Psalms had appeared to promise, to make Israel the top nation and send the wicked pagans back where they belong?' So: is this the time to restore the kingdom to Israel?

Many have assumed that Jesus' answer is 'No, but' – in other words, 'No, this isn't the time; that will come later; but you have work to do between now and then.' From that point of view, which has been popular in some quarters, not least within dispensationalism, 'restoring the kingdom to Israel' is a *further* goal, some way down the road, presumably involving some kind of national and geographical 'restoration' of the Judean people. That would make the disciples' witness 'to the ends of the earth' into a temporary fill-in, ahead of that eventual result. In that scheme, when the disciples ask, 'Is this the time for you to restore the kingdom to Israel?' Jesus' answer would be 'No, but': '*No*, it's not the time for that yet, *but* you have a job to be getting on with in the meantime.'

I have been convinced for many years that the correct answer is 'Yes, but'. Think again of the two on the road to Emmaus, who say, 'We were hoping that he was going to redeem Israel', with the implication that he was crucified, so he can't have been Israel's promised redeemer.[6] Jesus then explains that it was precisely through that event – his crucifixion – that his redemption would be accomplished. We should think back, too, to the parables of the kingdom, which say again and again, '*Yes*, the kingdom is indeed arriving, but *no*, it's not happening in the way you think.' It's like seeds planted in the soil . . . like a man with two sons . . . and so on. We might think also of Luke 19:11–27, when Jesus and his followers are approaching Jerusalem, the disciples think the kingdom will arrive immediately, and Jesus tells the parable about the nobleman coming back to see how his servants have got on with their commission. *Yes*, the kingdom is being launched right now; but *no*, it's not going to look like you thought.

---

6 Luke 24:13–35, at v. 21.

Think, too, of what Jesus told his followers at the Last Supper: that he wouldn't drink with them again until the kingdom of God arrived.[7] Clearly, for Luke (as indeed for all the others), the events of Jesus' death, resurrection and ascension really are the inauguration of his kingdom. The mission of the Church is not about *preparing for Jesus to become king*. It is implementing the fact that *he has become king*, even if that new kingship doesn't look like the sort of thing people had been expecting.

How does that work? We shall return to verses 6–8 in a moment. But for me the crunch comes in verses 9–11, where Jesus is taken up to heaven. If we ask, 'What is the most obvious and vivid scriptural account of God's kingdom being given to God's people?' the answer is of course Daniel 7 – which is itself a kind of nightmare version of Psalm 2, about the nations raging and then God exalting the Messiah. In Daniel, the four beasts do their worst, and then 'one like a son of man' is exalted on the clouds to sit beside the Ancient of Days, receiving kingdom, power and authority, so that all peoples, nations and languages should serve and obey him (verse 13, RSV). In Daniel 7 itself, this vision is interpreted in relation to 'the people of the holy ones of the Most High', in other words, the remnant of true Israel. Daniel 7 – focused on the 'one like a son of man' being taken up to heaven – is all about *the kingdom being restored to Israel*. What we have here in Acts 1 is the exaltation of the one Luke's readers have come to know as, inter alia, 'the son of man'. This exaltation is then followed at once, in Acts 1:15–26, by a careful description of the restoration of the 'twelve', the symbolic representatives of the renewed Israel, after the departure of Judas. Luke is saying, quite deliberately, 'This is what Daniel was talking about.'

We might notice, in parallel to this, that at the end of Matthew 28, in the so-called 'Great Commission' passage, the risen Jesus speaks of 'all authority in heaven and on earth' being 'given to' him, in words that echo those same promises in Daniel.[8] The whole New Testament is actually clear and unanimous: the sovereign rule of

---

7   Luke 22:18.

8   Matthew 28:18; Daniel 7:14, 18, 27.

Jesus, as king of the Judeans and hence lord of the world, is not post-poned until his eventual return (which of course is still in mind). It is truly inaugurated with the events of his death, resurrection and ascension. Nor should we understand Jesus' promises about his kingdom to refer to 'the end of the world', as many have thought. They are about God's good world *now under new management*. The second coming will complete the work, but it has now decisively begun. 'He has to go on ruling', says Paul, 'until "he has put all his enemies under his feet"'.[9] There is a future completion; but the 'rule' has already begun.

So we come back to verse 6. What did the disciples have in mind? We might think of the kingdom-movements in the centuries either side of Jesus. In the 160s BC Judas Maccabeus and his men overthrew the Syrian tyrant who had desecrated the Temple, and established an independent Judean kingdom which lasted for a century until the arrival of the Romans. In the 130s AD Simeon ben Kosiba, aka 'bar Kochba', was proclaimed as king, and ruled a small free kingdom for three years – until, once more, the Romans moved in. There were other kingdom-movements in between, par-ticularly in the 60s AD. Their task was always conceived in terms of overthrowing the Gentile idolators who had polluted the land and the Temple, and restoring God's people to be the pure torah-ob-servers they were supposed to be – quite possibly then becoming the supreme nation, ruling the world. It's not hard to see a straight line to that ambition coming from the Psalms and the Prophets: Israel's king will rebuild the Temple; he will be lord of the world; the princes of the nations will join themselves to Abraham's family; and that's how God will clean up and sort out the whole world.

So the disciples' puzzled question looks as though they are saying, 'Well, we weren't expecting all this, but now can we please get back to the main story, the great national dream?' And in that question they themselves were involved: like James and John earlier, they, presumably, expected to play key parts in that new work.[10] So Jesus

---

9   1 Corinthians 15:25. I have discussed this fully in *HE*, ch. 4.

10   See e.g. Mark 10:35–40.

is saying – and the whole of Acts is saying – *Yes*, this dream is now being fulfilled, but *No*, not in the way the disciples imagine. Their task is precisely to advance the kingdom *by being his witnesses*. In and through their work, the sovereign rule of the risen Jesus will become a reality on earth as in heaven. It will start small but it will quickly reach extraordinary new proportions. They must not, as Jesus indicates, bother their heads about when exactly the kingdoms of the world will finally become the visible kingdom of God and of Jesus. That's God's job. They are to get on with working *for* the kingdom – in other words, making it known in word and practice that Jesus is the world's new king. When Paul and Silas are later accused of saying that there is 'another king, Jesus', we shouldn't be surprised.[11] Luke wants to say, 'Well, yes, of course.' And this, as we shall see, raises the big question that haunts much of the narrative, and ought to be carefully pondered by all readers of Acts today: how does obedience to God, and the following through of this missionary mandate, play out in relation to human authorities?

We note already that the disciples' calling is to announce and inaugurate Jesus' sovereign rule. This will come into effect through their witness to him, their summoning people to repentance and faith (in other words, the people are to turn from idols and give allegiance to the one God), and their assuring them of salvation in the renewed world that will be completed at Jesus' return. But – and this is always hard for some Christians today to take on board – this isn't about explaining to people what they must do (or not do) in order to ensure that they will go to heaven when they die. You see, when we read the language of 'salvation', our minds easily flick back into the default mode of Western Christianity: we assume that the whole message is about 'going to heaven'. That is never mentioned here. In fact, *the New Testament isn't about our going to be with God; it's about God coming to be with us*. Think of the strapline in the last great scene of the Bible: not 'humans have gone to dwell with God', but 'God has come to dwell with humans'.[12] Luke, after all,

---

11 Acts 17:7.
12 Revelation 21:3.

regularly uses the language of 'salvation' to refer to what we might call 'this-worldly' realities, such as healings, or rescue from disaster including shipwreck. The point is that such events *anticipate* in the present time the ultimate rescue from death itself that is promised in the final new creation and resurrection.

Verse 8, then, sketches the sequence which the whole book will follow: Jerusalem and Judea, then Samaria as in chapter 8, and then the wider Gentile world, as in chapters 13 – 28. And with that we move to the climax of the passage.

The son of man coming in his glory

Generations of Western Christians have been puzzled by the ascension.[13] We have lived in an implicit cosmology in which 'heaven' is thought of as a long way away, up in the sky – reflected in hymns which speak of 'beyond the blue' and so on, and in stained-glass windows which have Jesus going upwards, with his feet sticking downwards out of a cloud. But with the rise of modern science people have realised (as many people in the ancient world knew, too) that heaven cannot be a location within our space–time universe, somewhere you would eventually get to if Elon Musk or Richard Branson flew you far enough. So what is the ascension about? Does it commit us to a kind of Jesus-the-spaceman viewpoint which we know to be deeply misleading?

No. The problem is with our implicit metaphysic and cosmology.[14] Modern secularism has assumed that, because there isn't such a place as 'heaven' within our cosmos, it can't exist. Many Christians in response have lurched towards Plato and said, 'Ah, but we have souls, and the soul's true home is "heaven", which is a "spiritual" place, not material at all.' That is the view, perhaps, of a majority of Western Christians today, insofar as they have reflected about the question.

---

13 See my *SH*, ch. 7.
14 On this paragraph and its wider implications see my *HE*.

But then we have . . . the ascension. Which is precisely about Jesus' *physical* body – his resurrected body, yes indeed, still recognisable by the mark of the nails, still able to walk and talk and, as in verse 4, to sit at table and eat with his friends. The ascension is about *this physical body* now being in 'heaven'.

This makes no sense in modern secular cosmology. But in the genuinely biblical cosmology it makes all the sense in the world. The difference between these two ways of understanding the world has nothing to do with the biblical cosmology being 'ancient' and the secular one 'modern'. Secular modernism is simply a new variation on ancient Epicureanism, in which the gods lived in a totally different sphere from the humans.[15] Most people in our culture, including most Christians, don't realise that there *are* different cosmologies; so most go along with the modernist one, without really thinking it through. Most Christians then add in a dash of Platonism, claiming that, even if we and God are a long way apart, we have souls which can jump the gap and which will eventually end up leaving 'earth' and going to 'heaven'.

That is an unbiblical distortion. In Scripture, from Genesis 1 onwards, *heaven and earth are the twin halves of God's good creation.* They are designed to interlock and overlap. They are made for each other. Scripture affirms repeatedly that they are designed eventually to come together as one. Heaven is God's space; earth is our space; but that isn't to suggest that 'heaven' is a *Platonic* heaven in which space, time and matter have no place. Far from it. To do cosmology, as with everything else, we should not start with other views of how the cosmos works and then try to fit Jesus into them. We should put Jesus at the centre, and rethink everything around him. With the ascension, the human body of Jesus is gloriously at home in his father's territory, against the day when he comes again to bring everything to judgement and to the long-awaited universal restoration, of which Peter speaks a couple of chapters later (3:21).

It's interesting that both Paul and John, when speaking of that moment, refer not simply to Jesus' 'coming', as though from some

---

15 See *HE*, ch. 1.

distance away, but to Jesus' *appearing* or *being revealed*. This is the language used in Colossians 3:4 and in 1 John 3:2. Heaven and earth are already secretly intertwined, with the heavenly reality – focused on Jesus himself – very close, but hidden as it were behind a curtain, ready to be revealed. The ascension isn't about Jesus going away and leaving us to our own devices. It's about Jesus now at the father's right hand – in other words, holding the place of authority and power in the whole cosmos. In the Bible, *heaven is the CEO's office*, the place from which things are run. And God made the world in such a way – as in Genesis 1 – that it would work properly when God's sovereign authority was put into operation *through obedient humanity*. That's what Psalm 8 is about – and Psalm 8 was very important in early Christian thinking, about our human destiny and calling but more specifically about Jesus himself. Jesus is now enthroned in the place of authority marked out for the human one from the beginning.

This is why the disciples, faced with Jesus going away, are not sorrowful, but joyful. Jesus is now lord of the world! He is now in charge! That's the good news! The one whose resurrection has launched the new creation, following his defeat of evil on the cross, is now ruling the world! And with that, in verse 11, the disciples enter the new time frame, the time between ascension and Parousia: 'This Jesus', declares the angel, 'will come back in the same way'. He will come, not to snatch his people away from earth as in some wrong-headed modern schemes, but to conclude the work of putting all things in subjection under his feet.[16]

The grand opening scene of Acts 1:1–11 then gives way to the rest of the chapter, which has to do with the vital reordering of the community of Jesus' followers. They begin as a fellowship of *prayer* in verses 12–14, the fellowship consisting of the Eleven, plus others including Jesus' mother and brothers. We notice already that, though the Twelve were clearly all men, the women were included in the new gathering from the start. And out of that prayer, in

16 So e.g. 1 Corinthians 15:20–8; Philippians 3:20–1. See the discussion in *SH*, ch. 8.

verses 15–26, comes what was obviously vital to them and indeed to Luke in telling this story. The Twelve must become twelve once again, after the tragic failure of Judas. This speaks volumes about the sense in the early community – and for Luke, placing this incident here – that the work of Jesus was all about the fulfilment, and the restoration, of God's ancient people, now indeed turning into their outward-facing mission to the world. Clearly the Twelve remained enormously important at the symbolic heart of the community, because it was vital that they were not an entirely new movement, not a strange idea that someone had invented, but the full flowering of God's ancient call of Abraham and his family. Peter's reference to the Psalms has the same function as the long 'backstory' in Stephen's speech in Acts 7 and Paul's initial discourse in Acts 13: to make it clear that what's now happening is what was always intended. And Peter, even before the gift of the spirit at Pentecost, is not only the spokesman and chief teacher, but also the scriptural exegete, locating through Scripture not only the failure of Judas but also what to do about it. Someone else must take his place.

And so they pray; they cast lots; and they choose Matthias. The fact that we hear nothing more about him is not significant. It reminds us, in case we thought otherwise, that Acts is very selective. It isn't providing a complete and rounded 'early church history', with all the varied detail we might want.

Conclusion

I now want to draw this first chapter together by briefly stressing five things that emerge from this passage and which must shape our reading of the rest of the book – and, with that, our own calling and mission under Jesus' lordship.

First, what biblical reference-points would first-century Judeans think of when faced with Jesus' ascension? They might think of Elijah, taken up to heaven in a whirlwind having promised Elisha that if he saw it happening he would receive a double share of his spirit.[17] Well, that's certainly how this story works as well. They might think of Moses going up the mountain to God, in order then to come down with the law. That's part of it too: Pentecost was seen by some Judean teachers as the feast of the giving of the law. And, as I've said, they would recall Daniel 7. The son of man has arrived on the clouds, to be enthroned in the place of executive power at God's right hand. All of these are part of the first-century Judean meaning of Acts 1.

But second, we need to consider – as we shall be doing in later chapters – what it means to say that Jesus is already ruling the world. People will say, as they've always said: 'Look at the world around you; just look out of the window! It doesn't *look* as though Jesus is in charge.' But think what we are saying. It is *Jesus*, not Caesar, not Herod, who's in charge. As Jesus made clear in Mark 10 and John 19, there is a sharp contrast between two different types of ruling, of authority. The rulers of this world stamp their will on their subjects by bullying and violence. Jesus wins the victory through the power of self-giving love. His followers will have to do the same: through their suffering, their martyrdom, their loving witness, their creation of communities that, by their very existence, call the world to account. The results are mostly not instantaneous. That's not how self-giving love works. But they will quickly be remarkable . . .

Acts describes the start of that often faltering process. The Church in every generation is called to carry it on. This isn't about a steady, smooth 'progress' of the gospel. That idea, an attempt to read the gospel through the lens of Hegel's philosophy, died a death (or should have done) a hundred and more years ago. But real gospel work continues, shaping communities and individuals through the witness of love and the power of the spirit. As historians recognise – I'm thinking particularly of Tom Holland's remarkable book, *Dominion* – the world is now already a very different place from the amoral darkness of the Roman Empire. Key differences can be traced to the Jesus-movement. Secularism tries to deny it, but it's true. One obvious example is the abandoning of unwanted

---

17 2 Kings 2:1–14.

children, especially baby girls. Everyone in the ancient world did this, except for the Judeans. But the Christians, in this as in other things, went with the Judeans – because they, too, were creational monotheists, believing that the present creation is the good work of the good Creator, and that humans are made in his image. And if today the vast majority of people in the world take the same line, that's an indication of a moral sea-change. There are many other examples.

Third, what would people in Luke's non-Judean world think of when faced with a story of someone ascending to heaven? After Julius Caesar's death, someone was bribed to swear that he had seen Caesar's soul ascending to heaven. That trick was repeated with many of the subsequent emperors. It meant that the emperor had now officially been 'deified' – so that their successor became 'son of the deified Julius' or whoever. This was a rather obvious way of solidifying Rome's hold on its vast empire. Now, to be sure, there are big differences. Jesus was now alive in a resurrection body, not a soul. Caesar had not been crucified! But the Roman world would get the point. The early church's belief in Jesus' ascension is foundational for their belief that there was indeed 'another king', as Paul and Silas are accused of claiming later on.

This is yet another way in which Acts chapter 1 looks ahead all the way to the close of the book. Think how it works. Acts divides at the end of chapter 12. In chapters 1 – 12, Jesus is hailed as king of the Judeans; and the present king of the Judeans – one of the Herods – comes to a bad end. Then, in chapters 13 – 28, Jesus is hailed as lord of the world . . . and what do we think will happen in Rome when the gospel arrives? That is the open question at the end of Luke's book. And for his readers today.

Fourth, a contemporary sideswipe. Those in my (Anglican) tradition, and in some others, will know that the Church recently decided to keep a feast called 'Christ the King' on the last Sunday before Advent, in late November. (I know many readers will not belong to traditions that observe the church year the way my tradition does, but I hope the point will be comprehensible.) The modern feast of that name was invented by Pope Pius XI in 1925, to counter the rise of Fascism. The Roman Church moved it to the last Sunday before Advent as recently as 1970. But having such a feast at that point in the Church's year reinforces the false view that Jesus only finally becomes 'king of the world' at the very *end* of the process, right before the second coming (to which Advent looks forward). But that undermines the whole gospel message. *We already have a 'feast of Christ the King'.* It is called Ascension Day – forty days after Easter. Pushing that celebration to the very end of the Church's year makes it look as though we don't understand what the ascension itself was all about. All our work and worship takes place under the present reality of Jesus as the world's true lord.

But fifth, a vital point which resonates forwards into the rest of the book: Jesus, in his human body, is now equally at home on earth and in heaven, so that in him the project of creation itself is fulfilled. In Ephesians 1:10, Paul declares that God's plan always was to unite all things in him, things in heaven and things on earth. With the ascension, part of earth – Jesus' body – is already and rightly in heaven. But if there is a physical place where heaven and earth come together – well, that is the very definition of a *temple*. A temple is a heaven-and-earth place, with an image of the god at its heart. Jesus is now that place, that image, that heart.

So if, in the first chapter of Acts, we see a small part of 'earth' – namely the human body of Jesus – fully at home in heaven, joining the two in himself, then in the second chapter we shall see the breath of heaven rushing down to fill the disciples. That is again Temple-language. *Acts 1 and 2 constitute Jesus and his people as the true Temple*, the place where now, already, God and humans, heaven and earth, come together. We will pursue this in the next chapter, when we're looking at Pentecost itself.

That is why, as we shall see, most of the pressure points and controversies in Acts are precisely about temples – whether in Jerusalem, or Athens, or Ephesus, or back again in Jerusalem. That is exactly what we should expect, and it shapes much of Luke's story. And temples are places of power and danger. If Acts is about the new Temple clashing with the old ones, this means a challenge of power. Who is really in charge, and how must Jesus' followers navigate this strange new world of competing power-claims? Acts calls us to discern, for our own time and place, what it means to live as the new Temple, confronting the idolatrous temples of our own day; and also what it means to say that we must obey God rather than human authorities. These all go closely together, as we will shortly see in what follows.

2

Acts 2 – 4

The New Temple

Introduction

The glorious scene Luke describes in Acts 2 is of course the day of Pentecost. Now most people today associate the word 'Pentecost' with the Pentecostal churches and the particular experiences for which they are known, especially speaking in tongues. When I was in my teens, they were very much in the minority in the UK. I well remember the double shock I had around the age of 20 when, first, a close relative came home from a year-long mission trip having begun to speak in tongues; and then, second, I fell in love with a girl who had been brought up in one of the classic Pentecostal churches. I soon learned quite a lot. And now, of course, the Pentecostal movements, and the cognate charismatic movements, have become much more mainstream. They have made substantial contributions to historic Anglicanism and also Roman Catholicism – much to the alarm of some in both denominations. But I think many of us have realised that God can and does do all kinds of remarkable things that burst out of our previous imaginations: new things that don't fit the safe patterns of our earlier theology and spirituality.

Pentecostal and charismatic theology, rooted partly in the nineteenth-century 'holiness' movements, have often focused on the idea of a 'second blessing'. The point would be that someone might have an initial experience of conversion, but that at some later date they might find themselves caught up by – or filled in a new way by – the holy spirit, lifting them (so it would seem) on to a new level of Christian experience. Those who have taught, and sought to foster, such 'second blessings' have often appealed to passages in Acts, not least to this chapter, suggesting that the disciples were already devout followers of Jesus but that they then needed, as a second stage, to be filled with the spirit, with all that might follow from that.

It seems clear to me, however, that questions such as these have to do with very modern analyses of spiritual formation, in which Luke simply isn't interested. He is not laying out different stages in the apostles' spiritual development. He is talking about the birth-day of the Church. And, as often happens, when people draw on a passage to make points which the passage itself isn't actually about, the main point that the writer is trying to make easily gets ignored. Thus discussions of Pentecostal and charismatic phenomena, frustratingly, have often not noticed what Luke himself thought that first Pentecost was all about.

God fulfilling his promise to dwell with his people

Luke signals his main point right at the start of Acts 2, and then in the full sweep of the chapter, together with chapters 3 and 4. He anchors his picture of Pentecost firmly in Scripture; and the scriptures he uses are not talking about levels or stages of 'Christian experience'. They are, if we can put it like this, about *God's own* 'experience'. The great overarching story of Scripture (to repeat a point already made) is not about how humans get to go upstairs and live with God. It is about God's intention to come and live *with* us and even, as we shall see, *in* us. So the point of Pentecost is not simply God giving his people a fresh injection of spiritual energy so that they can evangelise, teach, perform remarkable healings and so on. The point is *the homecoming of God*: God is doing at last what he had long intended and promised. Having come in the person of his son to fulfil the messianic predictions, God now comes in the person of his spirit to fulfil the even more personal promise to dwell in and with his people.[1] And thereby – as Luke is telling us by the way he has laid out this narrative – he renews the covenant with Israel and launches its original worldwide purpose.

Now all that's quite a mouthful. Those are not the categories most modern Christians, including charismatics, have used. But it is what Luke is talking about. So how does it all work out?

I said in the first chapter that, in Acts 1, heaven and earth are joined together in a new way, with a part of earth – Jesus' physical body – now being exalted in heaven. Now, in Acts 2, we see the breath of heaven coming to animate people on earth. This joining of heaven and earth, the very thing for which Jesus taught his followers to pray, fulfils God's original intention. It brings together the two halves of his creation in a new, rich unity.

With this we have to take a deep breath, and learn to think in the way people in the ancient world regularly thought. In the ancient world, except for some philosophers such as the Epicureans, the abode and activity of the gods and the abode and activity of humans were potentially involved with each other. That was often confusing and frequently dangerous. But this overlap of spheres was crystallised and symbolised in the building of temples. A temple, as we already saw, is basically a place where heaven and earth come together, a place where this or that god would dwell, and make his or her presence known to worshippers, and where devotees would come to worship, to pray, to offer gifts and sacrifices. And, of course, a temple would have, at its heart, an image of the god, giving worshippers a focus for their devotion and enabling the power of the divinity to be present and active.

Once we've got that straight, we need to go back to Genesis. In Genesis 1 creation itself is a temple: a heaven-and-earth structure *with an image at its heart.*[2] The image there is of course the human animal, male and female together. God's project in creation was to

---

1   E.g. Isaiah 52:8; Ezekiel 43:1–5; Zechariah 8:3; Malachi 3:1.

2   For this point and what follows, see esp. *HE*, ch. 5.

make a world in which he would come himself to be at home with his image-bearing human creatures.

Notice what follows. When it all went horribly wrong, God didn't abandon that project. He was still determined to live among his human creatures, and to call them to be 'image-bearers', reflecting his purposes into the world. God called Abraham and his family to launch his fresh heaven-and-earth project. How would that work? Well, cutting a long story very short, he rescued his people from slavery in Egypt at Passover. Then, on Mount Sinai, he gave Moses the gift of torah, and also the blueprint for the tabernacle. The torah prepared the people to be the tabernacle-bearing people, those in whose midst the living God comes to dwell; and the tabernacle itself was constructed as a statement of divine intent. It was a small working model of new creation. And in Exodus 40, God came to dwell there, to fill the newly made tent with his glorious presence.

Now in some (admittedly later) Judean traditions Pentecost – fifty days after Passover – was the feast of the giving of the law. It is quite possible that this link was already familiar to Paul and others. Luke, who understands so well why Jesus chose Passover for his climactic kingdom-inaugurating action, appears to understand equally well what the spirit is now doing.

The whole Bible tells the story of God fulfilling his original intention of coming to live with his people. In Exodus 40, the divine glory comes to dwell in the tabernacle. After David has settled the kingdom in Jerusalem, his son Solomon builds the temple that will replace the mobile tabernacle. It too is to be a small working model of God's eventual new creation; all these are pointers forward to the ultimate restoration of all things. And so, in 1 Kings 8, the divine glory comes to dwell in Solomon's newly built temple, as it had in the tabernacle in Exodus 40. We recall as well how, in Isaiah 6, the prophet sees the house filled with the smoke of God's presence.

Part of the point of these is *eschatological*: they all look ahead to promises such as those in Isaiah 11 or Psalm 72, where – through the Messiah's work – the whole earth is to be filled with the knowledge, or the glory, of God as the waters cover the sea. *The filling of the house points ahead to God's flooding of all creation with his glorious presence.*

That is the depth-dimension of the tragedy that strikes when, through Israel's persistent idolatry and sin, God allows the Babylonians to come and destroy the Temple itself. God had abandoned it, says Ezekiel.[3] The prophets (Isaiah, Ezekiel, Zechariah, Malachi) promised that he would come back.[4] But nobody in the Second Temple period ever said that this divine return had actually happened at last. (Indeed, if it had, one would assume that the pagans would no longer be in charge.)

Pentecost as the great turning point

That is the story – the open-ended story – which, in the Gospels and Acts, now suddenly reaches a new and decisive moment. *The New Testament declares that God has come back at last.* In Jesus, God has come back to judge and to rescue. In the spirit, God has come back to dwell in and with his people – as the advance sign and means of his eventual filling of all creation with his presence and love. That is the story we are now picking up.

The four Gospels – most obviously John, but actually all four in different ways – tell how this hope was fulfilled, close up and personal, in Jesus himself. The Word became flesh and *tabernacled* in our midst, and we gazed upon his glory.[5] Matthew says the same thing in his own way: Jesus is the Immanuel, God with us.[6] And now Luke is saying, here in Acts 2, 'This is what is now happening with the spirit.' The house is *filled* with the rushing wind; Jesus' followers are *filled* with God's personal empowering presence. Luke so wants to emphasise this notion of 'filling' that he opens the chapter

---

3 Ezekiel 10:1–22.

4 See n. 1 above.

5 John 1:14.

6 Matthew 1:23; 28:20.

by saying that the day of Pentecost itself 'had *fully* come'.[7] The idea of the rushing wind in verses 2–4 filling the house echoes the filling of the Temple in Isaiah 6, 1 Kings 8 and Exodus 40, as well as alluding to the creator spirit in Genesis 1:2. And the point, putting together Acts 1 and 2, is this: *Jesus and his people together constitute the new Temple*, the heaven-and-earth place, the launching of new creation.

This, to say it again, explains why most of the controversies in Acts, starting in chapters 3 and 4, are to do with temples. The story moves from the Jerusalem Temple to the pagan temples on the mission field, particularly in Athens and Ephesus; and then back to Jerusalem again.

So the powerful wind filled the disciples, enabling them to become, right there, the prototypes of the missionary Church. As has often been pointed out, the extraordinary phenomenon of 'tongues' is, at one level at least, a reversal of the disaster of Babel. Babel in Genesis 11 is the ultimate low point after the Fall of Genesis 3, the first murder in Genesis 4, and the wickedness and arrogance of the whole human race thereafter. The story of Babel itself has something of the shape of Psalm 2 and Daniel 7. The arrogant humans do their own thing, trying to rule the world their way. God laughs at them, and declares that he will confuse their languages so they can't understand one another. He is, meanwhile, calling and commissioning his servant to sort everything out. In Psalm 2, that is the Davidic king. In Daniel 7, it's one like a son of man. In the Babel story (Genesis 11), it's the call of Abraham in Genesis 12.[8] And so Pentecost symbolically launches the worldwide mission from that day to this. Of course, there is a radical difference between Babel and Pentecost: at Babel, the many languages made communication impossible, whereas, at Pentecost, they enabled it. But the similarity – and with it, the strong hint at a world put right at last – remains striking.

---

7   In *NTE* I translated this 'had finally arrived', but the Greek uses the same 'filling' root as in the subsequent verses.

8   Compare too e.g. Isaiah 41:29, leading to 42:1: God's answer to the chaos among the people is, 'Here is my servant, whom I uphold.'

So the gift of tongues, of being able to be understood across all language groups, has nothing to do with people reaching a new level of spiritual maturity. It is a sign of the global dominion of the risen and ascended Jesus. It is the launch of the worldwide Church, constituted then and there as the small working model of new creation. All nations can now hear in their own languages the mighty acts of God, and they will be called, as in Revelation 7, to praise God in those many languages. The early church is constituted as the single global family, the genuine article of which modern secular multiculturalism is a kind of parody. (But the latter phenomenon at least indicates a vestigial sense of what the Church was always supposed to be.)

All this, too, is of course rooted in Scripture. But in the Old Testament the sudden and effective gift of God's spirit was a special thing, confined to a few. What until now God had done in and through spirit-inspired people such as Moses, Aaron, Joshua, Gideon, Samson, Samuel, David, the prophets – this was now to be done through all his people.

Acts is not written, then, to describe *examples* of a 'normal process' of the spiritual development of individual believers. It is written to describe the one-off *inauguration* of a quite new reality. Pentecost, along with Good Friday, Easter and Ascension, constitutes the great turning point in the history of Israel and the world.

Peter's speech in Acts 2:14–46

Luke explains all this by reporting Peter's speech in Acts 2:14–46.

Peter describes the scriptural and theological depth of the events, at three levels. First, this is the long-awaited fulfilment of Israel's hopes: it is what we can summarise as the 'new covenant'. Second, this has happened through the scripture-fulfilling resurrection and exaltation of the crucified Jesus, Israel's Messiah. Third, it is therefore time for Israel to repent. This is itself a *covenantal* requirement, as in Deuteronomy 30: after the long years of exile, about which Israel was warned in Moses' great speech in Deuteronomy, there would come a moment when Israel would turn back, repent and be restored. That is what Peter is gesturing towards.

Again, none of these themes is concerned with the topics normally discussed in 'Pentecostal theology'. They are all about God's dramatic actions to bring Israel's history to its long-prophesied goal – indeed, to bring God's own story, the tale of his desire to dwell with and in his world, to its long-intended goal. God's filling of the house, and the disciples, is the new-Temple reality, pointing forward again to the ultimate future when God renews the whole world, as Peter says in the next chapter. This is the new map of world history.

You see, the question of what stage you or I may have reached in our own discipleship is a perfectly good question. But it simply isn't the question that the text is raising. That question comes to us from the past few centuries in the Western Church, with plenty of early-modern theorising about 'stages in the Christian life'. But the early church hadn't got that far yet! They were still being knocked off their feet by the one-off events that had just taken place. And if we are concerned, as we should be, for our own spiritual health, it is vital that we learn to see ourselves in the same way. We live, under the rule of Jesus, between covenant fulfilment and cosmic renewal. The gift of the spirit makes us living examples of the former (covenant fulfilment) and signposts to the latter (cosmic renewal). Welcome to the missionary Church.

So Peter claims that the prophecy of Joel is now fulfilled in the spirit's outpouring and the disciples' sudden multi-lingual gospel proclamation. This idea of spirit-driven renewal goes closely with themes we find in Isaiah, Jeremiah and Ezekiel.[9] They all look back, as I said, to the promise of renewal in Deuteronomy 30, following the long-range prophecies of blessing and curse in Deuteronomy 28 – 29. This is where the primal history of Israel was always supposed to turn its great corner. The later Old Testament writers see the whole history of Israel as a single long narrative, reaching the point where Daniel 9 predicts that the Babylonian exile – the time when pagans are still ruling over Israel because of Israel's idolatry

---

9   E.g. Isaiah 59:21; Jeremiah 31:33–4; Ezekiel 36.27; 37:14; Joel 2:28–9.

and sin – will last, not for seventy years, as Jeremiah had said, but for 'seventy times seven'. That half-millennium has now run its course. After the long exile under the rule of Babylon, Persia, Egypt, Syria and now Rome, as in the warnings that stretch from Deuteronomy to Daniel, it is time for the covenant to be renewed. And this of course has enormous implications for the relation between Jesus' followers and their fellow Judeans. That forms one of the ongoing subplots of Acts as a whole.

So Peter's first point is the renewal of the covenant, as in Joel, emphasising that this is for the personal renewal of *all* God's people, not only some: male and female, young and old. Peter's exposition of Joel, about the sun and the moon being darkened, may even have been occasioned by the darkness at noon as Jesus was crucified (mentioned in all three Synoptic Gospels), though Luke was as well capable as anyone of understanding biblical symbolic language and knowing that it refers to great and shocking events in the world of peoples, cities and nations. One way or another, the point, as in Joel, is that now 'everyone who calls on the name of the Lord will be saved' (verse 21). And here, as elsewhere in the New Testament, a prophetic text referring originally to YHWH now refers unambiguously to Jesus himself. In this moment of covenant renewal, the key marker for the rescued and renewed people will be their invocation of Jesus himself, who is now exalted, and who is now sending the spirit.

So if Peter's first point is the renewal of the covenant, his second is that this has happened precisely *through the victorious resurrection of the crucified Jesus*. The resurrection constitutes him as Messiah, as Paul insists at the start of Romans, alluding to 2 Samuel 7.[10] In Acts 2:22–36, Peter spells out in great detail how Jesus' bodily resurrection fulfils the messianic scriptures. Psalm 16 is particularly important, stressing the bodily incorruption which obviously had not been fulfilled in the person of the psalmist but which has now been fulfilled in Jesus.[11] This is one of the most emphatic texts anywhere in the New Testament about the empty tomb and the

---

10 Romans 1:3–4; 2 Samuel 7:12–14.
11 See Acts 2:25–33.

physicality of Jesus' resurrection. All this leads to the favourite early Christian text, Psalm 110, quoted in verse 34, where the exalted Messiah now begins his victorious reign. Then, in verse 36: 'God has made him Lord and Messiah – this Jesus, the one you crucified.' Looking later on, to Acts 4:11, Peter quotes from Psalm 118, as Jesus himself had done, seeing the Messiah as the stone which the builders rejected who is now the head of the corner. In other words, the Messiah himself *is* the true Temple.

First, new covenant; second, messianic victory; and third, the challenge to repent (verse 38). In these early chapters of Acts the people are urged to repent of the sin of rejecting Jesus as Messiah and his kingdom-message, and, more broadly, of the hard-heartedness that had caused that rejection. And the call to repent – to say it again! – brings into focus the theme of Deuteronomy 30, picked up in the prophets, not least Ezekiel and Daniel, about God's exiled people coming to their senses and turning back to him with all their heart.

As with John the Baptist's call to repent, this isn't just a matter of individuals turning from various sins, though that's obviously included. This is the long-awaited one-off moment, when Israel as a whole is to repent – and when that repentance will be the vital move in covenant renewal.

The call here is for the Judeans to turn back from the mindset which had caused them to reject Jesus and his peaceable kingdom-message. In Luke 19, Jesus had warned that the Romans would come and destroy the whole place because the people had refused to turn away from their idolatrous nationalism and embrace his kingdom-message of peace.[12] That is the force of Peter's challenge in verse 40. Let God rescue you from this wicked generation! As in Jesus' warnings in Luke 13:1–5, Peter here isn't warning about people going to hell when they die. He is picking up Jesus' warnings about the coming devastation of Temple, city and nation, and he is holding out following Jesus as the way of being forgiven (Acts 2:38) and so escaping that ruin. To be sure, this too broadens out in

---

12 Luke 19:42–4.

the early church into wider warnings, as for instance in Acts 17:31 where Paul tells the Athenian judges that the Creator God is calling all people to repent of idolatry and the sin it generates. But we must start with this historically specific focus.

So far then Peter has stressed the new covenant; Jesus the risen and exalted Messiah; and the call to repent. Then, in Acts 2:42–7, we see the new community taking shape. Verse 42 is often rightly seen as Luke's brief but fourfold definition of the early church: the apostles' teaching, the common life (*koinōnia*), the breaking of bread and the prayers. Teaching; fellowship; bread-breaking; prayer, with each flowing into the others. That's the wonderful rhythm that has sustained Jesus' followers from that day to this.

And this common life they began together was the life of a new *family*, in a world where 'family' meant helping one another, whatever need might arise. Clearly the sale of property didn't include the homes in which they lived and met. What mattered was living as a single new extended family. Verses 42–7 bring into focus what the whole chapter is about. *This is the new Temple*, the place where God is meeting with his people in grace. It was hugely attractive. Many were baptised and drawn into this sudden new movement.

When we put chapter 2 together, then, we find that the ancient promises about God filling the whole creation with his wisdom and glory have become focused on Jesus and his followers. The small sketch of the church in verse 42 functions eschatologically: Jesus' followers become *a small working model of the new creation*. When the text speaks of great awe, of powerful signs (presumably healings) and of celebration and praising God, this is what's going on: they are glimpsing the new creation itself, close up and personal. That remains the challenge for all Christian fellowships of whatever size or type.

Acts 3 and 4: Jesus as the fulfilment of Scripture

All this moves us swiftly in to Acts 3 and 4, where Peter and John invoke the powerful name of Jesus to heal a man who had been crippled from birth. This precipitates the first of many confrontations with the authorities. It frames a further explanation from Peter about the meaning of Jesus' death and resurrection (4:5–22) and then a dramatic prayer (4:23–30) which results (in 4:31) in a fresh shaking of the house and the disciples being freshly *filled* (there it is again) with the spirit. This last passage then completes a circle from the start of chapter 2. The house and its inhabitants are the focus of the divine drama – again, in implicit tension with the Temple itself. This theme holds these introductory scenes together.

As regularly in the Gospels, here in chapter 3 we have a dramatic action, a challenge, an explanation and a resulting controversy. In the Gospels, Jesus himself would explain, perhaps with a parable, what God was doing. Here in Acts it's the *disciples* who explain what *Jesus* was now doing, through the power of his name and his spirit. The Gospel story, remember, was about what Jesus had *begun* to do and to teach. Now we see what Jesus is *continuing* to do and to teach. That's the explanation for what's going on. So at the start of chapter 3, verses 1–11, Peter and John perform a dramatic healing of the man who'd been lame from birth. He was well known, and now everybody heard what had happened. For Luke, the healing is important but so of course is the explanation.

Once again, they tell the story. In 3:12–16, we have a dense statement that draws together three things. First (verse 13), Jesus has been glorified by Israel's God. This echoes Isaiah 52 and 53, where the Servant is 'handed over', but also 'exalted'. Second, Jesus died in place of a murderer (verse 14). Third, of course, God raised him to life. And fourth (verse 16), what has made the crippled man whole again is faith in Jesus' name. Luke doesn't here spell out the implicit Christology, nor does he spell out the implicit atonement theology, but it's all there in the scriptural echoes, especially those from Isaiah, issuing once more in the summons to repent. Jesus is the 'Prince of Life' (verse 15): that remarkable title sounds almost Johannine, suggesting that Jesus has life in himself, not just coming to life after his own death but being in charge, on God's behalf, of all life in creation.

These tight-packed verses look like a condensation of a much fuller account of Jesus and his death. As in the Gospel story, the combination of Isaiah's Suffering Servant and the historical account of Jesus dying in the place of the guilty says it all. This, however, is not the main point Luke wants to emphasise. He more or less assumes it, takes it for granted and moves on.

Peter now sketches more fully where they are in God's timetable (verses 20–1). He makes explicit, as the angel had done in Acts 1, the link between the ascension and Jesus' return. He has been taken into heaven until it's time for him to come back, at which point God will restore all things. But this means that the time has already arrived for the worldwide Abrahamic promises to become a reality, as Moses and the prophets had foretold (verse 25).[13] The promises to Abraham were made in the immediate aftermath of the disaster of Babel. Now, with Babel apparently reversed in Pentecost, those promises are at last to be fulfilled. In other words, the remarkable healing which has just happened points to Jesus as the personal fulfilment of Scripture. Now, says Peter, *you in turn* must become Scripture-fulfilling people, the true Israel that turns from sin and claims the covenant promise (25–6).

These massive claims constituted a direct affront to the Temple and its hierarchy, the official guardians of the national life. The chief priests are horrified that the disciples are proclaiming that 'the resurrection of the dead' has begun to happen in Jesus (4:2). Resurrection was already a revolutionary doctrine, which was why the aristocratic Sadducees opposed it: people who believed that kind of thing – well, there's no knowing what they might do in pursuit of their cause. (The Sadducees were well used to thinking this about the Pharisees; now they are faced with a whole new group talking about 'resurrection', and doing so in a whole new way.)

The idea, as in verse 2, that the general resurrection had begun with one person, in advance of all the rest, was an unprecedented modification in the doctrine. Orthodox Pharisaic belief was that all God's people would be raised from the dead in the end. (This may be one reason why Jesus' own unexpected resurrection caused Paul at least to conclude that Jesus was *representing* God's people

---

13 See e.g. Genesis 12:1–3; 17:4–6; 22:15–18.

in person; that he really was God's Messiah.) In any case, the claim made by Peter and the others, that the person who had been raised from the dead was the Jesus who had been crucified as a messianic pretender – this was a total shock. And, out beyond the specifics, as far as the chief priests were concerned the Temple was the place where God had promised to dwell, and to act to rescue his people. Who were these people claiming that the promises had been fulfilled in such a different way?

So they interrogate the disciples (Acts 4:5 onwards). 'What power did you use? What name did you invoke?' This might have been, perhaps, the prelude to a potential charge, that the disciples were using some kind of dangerous magic. Peter replies (in 4:8–12), as by now we expect, that Jesus' resurrection was God's vindication of him as Messiah, and – a poke in the eye for the present Temple-hierarchy – that he, Jesus, is the stone the builders rejected who is now the chief cornerstone. In other words, the disciples hadn't just been using some random magic name. This was the fulfilment of the very traditions the chief priests were claiming to represent! There follows in verses 13–18 the slightly comic scene in which the Temple-hierarchy try to insist that the disciples should not talk about Jesus any more. As if! Back comes the reply, opening a major theme in Acts to which we shall return: we must listen to God rather than to you (verses 19–20).

The leaders go back to join the others and tell them what's happened. This precipitates, in verses 23–31, one of the classic early Christian prayers. Solemnly invoking God the creator of all (verse 24), it moves into Psalm 2, a central source for early Christology. Psalm 2 begins, as they quote, with the nations raging and plotting. Yes, say the disciples, Herod plus Pilate plus the Judean leaders together represent the world's rulers. It was the greatest empire, and the finest religion, the world had ever known that together put Jesus on the cross. That is where they start.

But they're not just using the first two verses of the psalm as a peg on which to hang their prayer. As often in the New Testament, when you have one line or verse of Scripture being quoted, you should look at the larger context, which the writer or speaker may well be assuming. In this case it seems that Psalm 2 is, as it were, continuing to be 'heard' or imagined, just behind the spoken text. In the psalm, God laughs at the foolish world rulers, declaring that he has established his king on Zion – as we said before, rather like God laughing at the builders of Babel and then calling Abraham to begin the long journey of salvation. The prayer assumes that Jesus himself is the one now enthroned on Zion, named as God's son, receiving from his father the nations as his inheritance.

The psalm then concludes (Psalm 2:10) by addressing the world's rulers: 'Now therefore, O kings, be wise' (my emphasis). The prayer in Acts 4 picks up that phrase 'now therefore' and turns it into a new prayer in verse 29:

So now, Master, look on their threats; and grant that we, your servants, may speak your word with all boldness, while you stretch out your hand for healing, so that signs and wonders may come about through the name of your holy child Jesus.

That is the point at which, as at the start of chapter 2, the house is shaken, and the disciples are once again filled with the spirit. Once more they become a small working model of what God will do with the whole creation. The narrative of chapters 2, 3 and 4 has come full circle. The Pentecost people are launched into a dangerous but exhilarating new world.

This is where I want to say, to anyone reading this book: if you don't already know this prayer, get to know it. If you're engaged in any work for God's kingdom, any ministry of evangelism, teaching or pastoral wisdom, you're going to need it. Get to know Psalm 2, standing behind this prayer as it stands behind a good deal of Scripture, and learn how to enter into its spirit and apply it to new situations. Many times in ministry you will be preparing a sermon or talk, or engaging in one of a thousand important tasks, and something gets in the way – sometimes simply distractions, innocuous in themselves but gently pulling you away from your focus; sometimes more sinister, perhaps a sudden dark temptation; or perhaps an intervention from outside, a phone call from a senior parishioner warning you not to preach about a particular topic. Many times the Church is called to take a stand, and the local authorities – from a city councillor all the way up to the national political hierarchy – may send a clear warning that this is not wanted. This will happen more and more, especially in polarised political situations or places where the Church is under threat from the authorities.

Sometimes the warning may be wise and you may actually need it. The fact of somebody opposing you doesn't automatically mean you're in the right! But in all genuine kingdom-work there will be moments when you find yourself confronted with one kind of challenge or another. At that point, I strongly recommend that you go back to Psalm 2 and Acts 4, and cling on for dear life to the great conclusion:

> So now, Master, look on their threats; and grant that we, your servants, may speak your word with all boldness, while you stretch out your hand for healing, so that signs and wonders may come about through the name of your holy child Jesus.

The end of Acts 4 echoes both the gathering of the Church to pray in Acts 1:13–14 and the short summary of the church's life in 2:42–7. The witness to the risen life of Jesus (verse 33) was embodied in the radically new lifestyle of the disciples, living as family and sharing all they had. As a result (verse 34), 'there was no needy person among them' – which is a quotation from Deuteronomy 15:4, where Moses is predicting the blessing that will come upon the covenant people. That's part of the point: what they were doing was not simply random acts of kindness but the new lifestyle which constituted a fulfilment of torah itself. All this is part of the build-up, with the opposition of the Temple-hierarchy going on at the same time, to the implicit conclusion that it is in Jesus' followers that the traditions and hopes and life of ancient Israel, and the intertestamental Judeans, were now being brought to fulfilment. They were themselves, of course, all Judeans; there is no sense of replacing Israel with someone quite different. Luke is presenting the followers of Jesus as the people of the fulfilled covenant.

Conclusion

So where does this leave us, as followers of Jesus today? In these first four chapters of Acts, we have seen the establishment of the new Temple, the place where heaven and earth come together. The one God has come to his people in the person of the son, in whose very body heaven and earth are joined. This same one God has now come in the person of the spirit (or, to put it another way, Jesus has now poured out his spirit, as in Acts 2:33), to dwell with and even *in* his people, renewing them as covenant members and enabling them to bear powerful witness. God's filling of them with the spirit points ahead to his final filling and renewal of all things. And all this happens because Jesus, Israel's Messiah, is exalted to reign beside the father on the throne of the universe.

Of course, the world's rulers won't like it. If we take on this vocation, the principalities and powers – of whatever sort – will tell us to concentrate on heaven while they run the earth. Or they will warn us not to shove our religion down their throats, while they (of course) continue to shove their secular materialism and rampant hedonism down ours. We must not lose our nerve. We are people of the renewed covenant. We are the family of the Messiah, marked with his powerful name in our baptism. We are, not least, to be filled, and filled, and filled again with the spirit. We are called, corporately and individually, to be a sign and foretaste of the Creator God's ultimate purpose. In the meantime, our task is to lead the praises of Jesus himself, our crucified lord, risen, reigning, returning.

3
Acts 5 – 8

Mission and Martyrdom

Introduction

A quick skim through Acts chapters 5 – 8 plunges us into an apparently mixed bag of disparate and disturbing topics. The honeymoon of chapters 1 – 4 is over. The new-Temple movement has been launched . . . and now we come down to earth with a bump, with Ananias and Sapphira. Then there is a violent confrontation with the Temple-authorities; then squabbles about food-distribution to widows; and then Stephen's martyrdom. We then switch to Philip, dashing around – it seems at random! – in chapter 8. What's all this about?

We still have to address two outstanding questions that have emerged from the book so far. What exactly is the relationship between 'obeying God' and living under human authority? And what exactly were the early Christians thinking about the Temple – granted that they were constituting themselves as the real Temple, worshipping Jesus as the one who holds heaven and earth together, and so on, and yet were continuing to worship in the present Temple and meet in one of its large porticos? Granted that Jesus had denounced the present Temple and warned of its imminent destruction, why do they, and then later Paul, too, go on worshipping there? Why not abandon it altogether?

With questions like these, we today are inclined to go for an either/or. We vote *either* 'for' the authorities *or* 'against' them, and then either 'for' the Temple or 'against' it. That's because we are children of the Enlightenment, with its left/right polarisation and its urge to occupy extreme positions, rather than thinking like the early Christians, with their sense of inaugurated eschatology, with the inaugurated new age overlapping with, and actually challenging, the old as it awaits its final conclusion. We will circle back to these questions, because they aren't going away. As we move ahead in Acts we will be in a better position to give them the nuanced response they deserve. But I mention them here in case it might look as though we had left them behind by mistake.

Obeying God, not human beings

We begin, however, with chapter 5, plunging straight into the disturbing story of Ananias and Sapphira. It's small comfort to observe that this is a one-off. We don't (thank goodness) find other early disciples being struck dead because of their sin. Paul does warn, in 1 Corinthians 10 and 11, about the dangerous or even deadly consequences of casual participation in the Lord's Supper. He speaks cryptically but sharply in 1 Corinthians 5 of an immoral man being handed over to the satan for the destruction of the flesh. Those are striking enough. But there's nothing quite like this. Acts 5, like everything else in these early opening chapters, is vivid and instantaneous, with disturbing elements of final eschatology, negative as well as positive, rushing forward into the present.

There are obvious biblical parallels for the tragic scene. There are Aaron's sons, Nadab and Abihu, being struck down at once after offering 'unholy fire' (Leviticus 10). Then there is the wretched Achan in Joshua 7, suddenly tempted into covetousness, taking the devoted goods and suffering terrible consequences. There is the unfortunate and apparently innocent Uzzah in 2 Samuel 6, reaching out to steady the ark. All these incidents, we note, come in a cultic, not so much a moral, setting. They are not simply about doing something that was forbidden. They are about treating the things of God as though they are just ordinary. They are confrontations with the mystery of holiness.

This, it seems, is the risk you run in a temple, with the immediate presence of God. You want to be close to God? Well, watch out. That description of the common life at the end of chapter 4 – the sharing of possessions, the pooling of money – isn't just pragmatic. It's about being the new holy people, the Temple-people in whose midst God has come to dwell. I see a sort of parallel here to what we find at the start of Jesus' public career. Jesus' early kingdom-announcements, in the synagogues of Galilee, drew out of the woodwork all kinds of opposition: shrieking demons, suspicious Pharisees, plots from the Herodians and so on. So, too, the setting up of this new holy people, right next door to the Temple, seems to have been a magnet for satanic corruption. To this day, the early steps of a new vocation, or a new spirit-led movement, may well attract new pressures, anxieties and especially new temptations. I have seen this again and again.

At the heart of it – as often with satanic activity – was a *lie*. Ananias and Sapphira were under no obligation to hand over to the church all the proceeds of their property sale. They said they had, but they hadn't. Peter declares that they were lying to the holy spirit. At the heart of this is *holiness*: if the church is the new Temple, with God really in the midst, that means fear and trembling, not playing fast and loose. That applies in many areas, not just – though not least – with money. If we really are doing business with the Creator God, this isn't just a strange religious game. It is claiming, riskily, to be part of the ongoing life-giving project of the God who made heaven and earth.

As though by contrast with the shocking story of Ananias and Sapphira, Acts 5:12–16 give a further portrait of the growing church's daily life, focusing on remarkable healings, with people bringing their sick into the streets in the hope that perhaps even Peter's shadow would fall on them as he went by. But, as in chapter 3, these healings, and the church's growing reputation, precipitate another confrontation. The authorities (verse 17) are 'filled with righteous indignation', the Greek being *zēlos*. That's naturally translated as 'zeal'. But that doesn't simply mean a heated-up inner disposition. At that period, and in that culture, 'zeal' was almost a technical term for the urgent intent to enforce God's will through violence. No doubt the authorities would say they were jealous for the honour of God and the Temple. Why should they tolerate a ragtag group squatting right outside one of the huge main gates of the holy shrine? But we may surmise that there was also a very human jealousy, with the increasingly popular church meeting right there in Solomon's Porch. So they arrest the leaders and put them in prison overnight.

Verses 17–26 then give us the darkly comic scene of an angel releasing the apostles from their overnight prison stay. The guard who has been sent to fetch them reports that they're not there. Then someone else rushes in and declares that the apostles are already in the Temple itself, teaching the people. So they fetch them again (verse 26). Luke is making it clear that the authorities were now nervous of the public reaction if they visibly mistreated the apostles, who were obviously becoming quite popular. And this time they try to threaten them (verses 27–33), not least because, it seems, the apostolic message about Jesus hints, quite rightly, at the authorities' shared responsibility for Jesus' death. 'You're trying to bring this man's blood on us' (verse 28).

This is where (verse 29), Peter responds about obeying God, not human beings. He follows that up, in another Lukan summary (as in chapter 3), with a statement of the Gospel events. Verse 30: the God of our ancestors raised Jesus: in other words, this is what Abraham's God himself was doing. It wasn't some bizarre departure from our national heritage and hope. But yes, you, the authorities, had laid violent hands on him and hanged him on a tree. As in Jesus' words in John's Gospel, though the Romans who actually crucified Jesus bore their responsibility, the ones who handed him over to the pagans had the greater sin (John 19:11).[1] But God has now exalted him (verse 31) to his right hand (that's Psalm 110 again) as leader and Saviour – two titles that bring out different aspects of messiahship. And this has launched the new covenant, which has repentance and forgiveness at its heart.

---

1 Compare also Acts 4:27 where Herod, Pilate and 'the nations and the peoples of Israel' are said to have acted all together.

That, then, is Luke's summary. But it gives a fair indication of the repeated apostolic message. And, like Paul in Athens (as we'll see when we get to chapter 17), what's happened is that, though the apostles are before the Sanhedrin as prisoners on trial, they are turning the tables. It's now the Judean authorities who are on trial – before God.

That, of course, just makes things worse (verse 33). Anticipating their reaction to Stephen two chapters later, the authorities want to kill them.

Luke skates quickly over this, taking time instead in verses 34–9 to describe the intervention of the Pharisee Gamaliel. Gamaliel was a leading representative of the more 'lenient' branch of Pharisaism. Already by the time of Jesus, there were two distinct branches, engaging in sharp debate with each other. There were the followers of Hillel, who were regarded as being more 'lenient'; and there were the followers of Shammai, the more 'severe' or 'strict'. But what were they 'lenient' or 'strict' *about*? It's easy, reading later Judean texts, to think that they were lenient or severe about the personal observance of torah, with Shammai advocating a harsher regime and Hillel a gentler one. But far more was at stake than simply personal law-keeping. What mattered was figuring out what obedience to torah meant *in terms of resisting the rule of the pagans*. For Shammai, nothing less than out-and-out opposition was required. Following the Maccabees, one should be 'zealous for torah', which meant either direct or covert violent action. For the Hillelite faction, it was better to keep torah oneself but not to try to fight the Romans. This was the famous switch, as some have put it, from politics to piety; though the two factions were still arguing it out until the 130s, when the Shammaites backed bar Kochba in his revolt and were wiped out, leaving the more moderate Hillelites to carry forward what became the Judaism of the Mishnaic period.

All that is to say that Gamaliel, whom we meet in this passage but whose reputation lived on in the later rabbinic writings, was a classic Hillelite. 'Live and let live' was the motto, or at least 'Wait and see'. He points out that there are precedents for strange movements, most of which fall by their own weight. But, he says (verse 39), watch out – you might find yourselves fighting against God! And the Sanhedrin, who hold him in great respect, take his advice.

I think Luke describes this in detail because one of his subtexts all through the book is that this is the sort of conclusion that wise authorities ought to reach. Think of the magistrates in Philippi in chapter 16, or the town clerk in Ephesus in chapter 19. Or indeed of the Roman centurion in the sea voyage in chapter 27. Anyway, the Sanhedrin authorities back down. They limit their reaction to a beating and a warning. The apostles are not fazed. They, as good Judeans, know that suffering for the holy name is a privilege. This too acts not as a deterrent ('maybe we've been wrong!') but rather as a confirmation ('this shows we are the true, suffering people of God').

So with chapter 5 we have the *internal* threat to the church's dangerous holiness, and then the *external* threat from the Temple-authorities. This Temple-focus makes good sense of Acts, pointing out all kinds of lessons for us: the dangers of compromise on holiness, not least to do with money; and the discernment of when to say we must obey God, not human authorities. All this is part of learning to live as Temple-people in a conflicted and confused world, as people of new *creation* within the present ambiguous distorted creation, resisting the simplistic pseudo-holiness of a dualism that dismisses existing structures as hopeless. As I hinted before, we tend to grab for what looks like a 'pure' solution, because post-Enlightenment politics inclines us to think in that simplistic either/or fashion. That, I think, is because the secular Enlightenment was trying to get a kind of realised eschatology, making a new world, here and now, on the basis of human reason alone. But if you believe in God's inaugurated eschatology, you have to get used to living between the times, with a 'now' and also a 'not yet'. There's a lot there to ponder, not least as the Church ought to be giving a lead in our contested and fractious political times.

Temple and torah in God's longer purposes

Chapter 6 opens with an apparently quite different issue: a squabble between believers from different cultural backgrounds. The widows in one group seem to be better looked after in the daily food-distribution than those in the other group. Note in passing the huge innovation in social policy that Luke takes for granted: if you're going to live as extended family, you'll have to make careful arrangements for people who would otherwise be destitute. This reflects the Old Testament's regular concern for the orphan, the widow and the foreigner (an obvious example is Psalm 72, which is the more interesting as it is about the wise rule of the true king). That concern, picked up in the early church, has turned into a movement of social care which now, after two thousand years, is the assumed norm in most cultures.

Within that, however, there's a big problem, foreshadowing later ones. All those involved are Judeans. But in Jerusalem there were many groups of Greek-speaking Judeans, migrants from the wider Diaspora. Sadly but predictably, even in these early stages there was overt discrimination, perhaps not intentional but none the less noticeable, with the indigenous Aramaic-speaking widows being treated as first-class citizens and the incomers being relegated to the second class.

As with Ananias and Sapphira, this problem had to be nipped in the bud. The new family life must, by definition, transcend all boundaries of culture, language, background, and ultimately – though we're not quite there yet – ethnicity itself. So what's to be done? Things need to be run better . . . but not by the apostles, because they already have their work cut out with leading the community in prayer and the teaching of Scripture. (Luke calls this 'the ministry of the word', which seems to be both the 'word' of the gospel and the rootedness of that 'word' in Israel's Scriptures.) So the community prayerfully chooses seven people to run food-distribution, allowing the apostles to continue their work of prayer and Scripture-teaching.

The Seven have noticeably Hellenistic names. The last one, Nicolaus, is 'a proselyte from Antioch': in other words, he had been born as a Gentile, had converted to Judaism, and was now grasped by the gospel. So the Gentile question is already in sight. And this offers a practical symbol to those who felt they were being neglected.

All this brings us to Stephen, the first of these 'stewards'. (They are often referred to as 'deacons', but not in Acts itself.) He and Philip are appointed to look after widows and food, but they quickly develop quite different ministries. (Once you lay hands on people and pray for them, whether formally or informally, you have literally no idea what the spirit is going to do next.) Stephen turns out to be a powerful Scripture exegete and apologist, able to articulate and defend the gospel and its implications. Philip becomes an entrepreneurial evangelist. I suspect the other five had equally varied futures, though we don't get to hear about them. But we take Stephen first, from 6:8 onwards.

Here again the question of the Temple dominates. Verse 9: Stephen disputes with Hellenistic Judeans from North Africa and southern and western Turkey (Cyrene, Alexandria, Cilicia and Asia). What's going on? Why them? Well, why have they migrated to Jerusalem? Presumably to be near the Temple: they are devout Judeans and want to be near the place where Israel's God has chosen to dwell on earth. But now a new movement is claiming to upstage it! These Jesus-followers seem to be claiming that God is indeed dwelling on earth – but in a far more dynamic form, catching them up and doing new things. So they press the question to Stephen: What's going on?

They turn out to be no match for his wisdom and his spirit-given ability to expound Scripture. So they cut through that and frame a legal charge. Verses 11–14 show what it's all about. Verse 11: he was, they say, speaking blasphemous words against Moses and God. Verse 13: he's speaking against the holy place and the torah! Verse 14: 'Jesus the Nazorean will destroy this place' – that is, the Temple – and change the customs Moses gave us. That's all fairly damning stuff. What's it about? What had Stephen been saying?

Now, as in Jesus' trial before Caiaphas, Luke indicates that they call *false* witnesses. The charges are very similar to those levelled against Jesus himself, having to do with the Temple: is Jesus repudiating it? Will he destroy it? What then happens to the ancient promises that God will dwell there in the midst of his people?

In Jesus' trial, though, the falsehood was not a total fabrication. It was a matter of slant, of emphasis. After all, Jesus himself had said, in John 2, 'Destroy this Temple . . . and I'll raise it up in three days.' The Synoptics, especially Luke, are full of warnings against the present Temple, reaching a climax in Luke 21 and parallels, all leading to the mocking of Jesus on the cross ('you were going to destroy the Temple and build it in three days' (Matthew 27:40), and so on). All that makes sense once we realise that Jesus' kingdom-proclamation, and his own role within that, formed a *counter-Temple movement* – reaching its climax, as we've seen, in the ascension and Pentecost.

Such a movement made sense at the time. Qumran was a counter-Temple movement, though remaining content to wait quietly in the desert for God to act. In Luke 19, Jesus claimed to be embodying precisely that divine action. So Jesus had indeed warned that God would judge the Temple. Like Jeremiah who had said similar things half a millennium earlier, he was suspected of being either a false prophet or a disloyal Judean, or quite possibly both. But supposing God really was warning his people that their ongoing rebellion was going to precipitate cataclysmic judgement?

The problem then comes with the *interpretation* of that understanding of the Temple. Stephen's opponents, like some to this day, seem to have understood him to be saying that the Temple was a bad thing and that Jesus had launched a totally different movement. So too with the law of Moses (Acts 6:13–14). Jesus had insisted that he hadn't come to abolish the law but to fulfil it, but that could very easily be misunderstood – as generations of Paul-readers have misunderstood it – to mean that the Mosaic law was a bad thing now happily to be abolished. It is *that* misunderstanding, to this day, which leads people to ask why, if the disciples were a counter-Temple movement, they went on meeting in the Temple porch and worshipping in the Temple itself. Why not move somewhere else altogether? There's plenty of room down by the Dead Sea . . . ?

Stephen's answer is clear in chapter 7. The law and the Temple were good, God-given gifts, signposts to his eventual intention to fill all creation with his glory. But the hard-hearted people to whom law and Temple had been given didn't obey the law, and didn't

understand what the Temple was and wasn't. They did not realise that the Temple was all along a forward-looking signpost, and
that, when the reality itself dawned, the signpost would have completed its God-given task. That failure opened up the danger, as in
Jeremiah, that the hard-hearted people would want to idolise the
Temple itself, irrespective of their own attitudes and behaviour. This
is actually very close to what Paul says in 2 Corinthians 3. There,
the problem was not with torah itself, but with the hard hearts of
Moses' original hearers. It is also close to what Jesus says in Mark
10, where the reason Moses gave the command about divorce was
not because Moses was giving bad laws but because the people's
hearts were hard.

In order to work round to this point, Stephen does the usual
Judean thing. He tells Israel's story from Abraham on, in order to
make clear the substantial continuity of the Jesus-movement with
Israel's deepest traditions. The underlying charge (Moses, law,
Temple, even God!) is basically that Stephen and, through him, the
larger Jesus-movement are a dangerous departure from loyalty to
Israel's God. Not so, replies Stephen. Despite the accusations, he
endorses Moses, and points out that Moses himself had prophesied
an eventual successor (Deuteronomy 18). He explains that there
was nothing wrong with the angelically given Mosaic law, only
with the people, whose uncircumcised hearts and ears, like those
of his present hearers, couldn't receive it (Acts 7:51). And as for the
Temple: yes, tabernacle and Temple were gifts from God, but they
were pointers to a different reality, to the coming together of heaven
and earth, as in Isaiah (verses 49–50). Isaiah 66 had already challenged the idea that the Jerusalem Temple might be a permanent
fixture. Stephen is claiming the high ground of Scripture. He is not
rejecting the Temple, any more than the torah. He is explaining the
eschatological contextualisation of both Temple and torah within
Israel's ongoing story – which is now fulfilled in Jesus, the prophet
like Moses.

More particularly, he shows how Joseph, rejected by his brothers, was made ruler over all Egypt; then how Moses, rejected by
the Israelites in his first rescue-attempt, was called by God to go

back and rescue them in fact. This pattern has now repeated: the present generation rejected Jesus, but God has vindicated him. The way Stephen reaches this climax once more echoes Scripture. Jesus is 'the Righteous One', and they have killed him. It is rather like the scene at the start of the Wisdom of Solomon, and it's quite possible that Stephen, a highly educated Hellenistic Judean, knew that book.

Stephen is officially on trial; but his dramatic conclusion isn't a defence. Once again, as with the apostles two chapters earlier or with Paul in Athens later on, the speech was itself an accusation against the present hierarchy. They, like their ancestors, are resisting the holy spirit. Even this too, sadly, is a fulfilment of Scripture, which told the story *both* of God's overall purposes *and* of Israel's persistent rebellion. Acts 7 is a classic example of what we find again and again in the New Testament, though it's sometimes obscured when people today think of two 'religions' called 'Christianity' and 'Judaism' and compare them. The point Stephen was making, in line with so many other early Christians, was that following the crucified and risen Jesus was the true fulfilment of Israel's Scriptures. If that meant regarding even Temple and torah as God-given but strictly temporary institutions, so be it. And the opposition from Israel's official leaders was itself also predicted in Scripture.

But even as his judges gnash their teeth at his apparently arrogant insults, Stephen gazes up into heaven and tells them what he sees. We should by now recognise the Temple-overtones as well as the scriptural echoes: 'Look!' he says. 'I can see heaven opened, and the son of man standing at God's right hand!' Having denounced the present Temple and its rulers, Stephen himself is caught up for a moment within the total new-Temple reality. Still on earth, he gazes at God's glory: and there is Jesus, not now *sitting* at God's right hand, but *standing*. Jesus, as the true high priest, is interceding with God on behalf of his suffering people. Stephen's vision upstages the Temple and its hierarchy, rounding off his denunciation of the latter for their abuse of the former.

Now, we have many Judean martyr-stories from the period. The martyrs regularly call down God's curse on their persecutors, warning of swift divine judgement. Stephen breaks the mould.

'Lord,' he prays, 'don't let this sin stand against them.' This of course points back to Jesus himself in Luke 23:34 ('Father, forgive them! They don't know what they're doing!'). The Jesus who was right then interceding for Stephen (as in Romans 8:34) had taught him that intercession, rather than cursing, was the way of the new, fulfilled, law and Temple. This was a radical innovation indeed, a quintessential gospel moment, with God's forgiving love shining out even in the moment of death. And Stephen's personal prayer echoes that of Jesus: 'Receive my spirit' (verse 59) goes with 'Here's my spirit' in Luke 23:46. (It is interesting that they both refer to the 'spirit'; neither here nor elsewhere in early Christianity do we find people referring to the 'soul' in this connection, however common that Platonic idea has become today.[2])

Stephen's speech in Acts 7 therefore holds together this whole section of Acts. Jesus and his people are the new heaven-and-earth reality *to which the law and the Temple had pointed all along, even though this meant their ultimate relativisation.* Jesus is the true deliverer who, like Joseph and Moses, was initially rejected by the people. This new-Temple theology explains retrospectively the Ananias-and-Sapphira incident: those who handle holy things must treat them *as* holy, not as toys for their own pleasure. (Those of us who are ministers of word and sacrament should take note.) It explains the clash with the Sanhedrin: this is indeed the new Temple, even though Jesus' followers continue to worship in the old one. *Beware of the temptation to dualism,* to think that the only response to corruption is to get out and go elsewhere. Yes, there may come a tipping point. But hotheads – like young Moses in Egypt, or indeed young Joseph with his dreams! – often want to reach that point sooner than they should. Of course, Jesus did say that when 'the desolating abomination' is set up, his followers should get out and run. When Mark (13:14) quotes that, he adds, 'let the reader understand'. That's a word for all of us at difficult times.

---

2   See my book *FAS.*

The gospel reaches Samaria

So, we have the new Temple, the new Jesus-and-his-people reality. What has that got to do with Acts chapter 8?

Well, everything. As the authorities extend their persecution, and church members are scattered, they go off – and Philip goes to Samaria. For centuries now the Samaritans hadn't come to Jerusalem. They had their own temple on Mount Gerizim. But now Jerusalem comes to them! The gospel reaches out; and a people who are barred from the Jerusalem Temple, by the Judeans and by their own traditions, are embraced within the new heaven-and-earth reality. So when, in verses 14–17, Peter and John go to Samaria, this is not, please note, to bestow a 'second blessing' on them in the very modern sense, or indeed to 'confirm' them. Pentecostals have tried to make it the former; Catholics and Anglicans have tried to turn it into the latter. Both are wrong – because both are completely anachronistic. Those were not the issues at stake. Peter and John were making it absolutely clear that what was going on was *not* a new, separate movement – which might quickly have led to there being a Jerusalem church on the one hand (or indeed a *Judean*-only church), and then a Samaritan one on the other. Many at the time would have heaved a sigh of relief at such a tacit separation. Let them be a different 'denomination'. If they've planted a new church, good luck to them, but we're not going to want to have too much to do with them! After all, they're Samaritans and we're Judeans . . .

Wait a minute! That's not how God's gospel works. As with the multicultural, though still Judean, widows in chapter 6, it is vital that the Samaritan believers are seen and known as *part of the same family*. The outpouring of the spirit makes that clear. This is what Paul is driving at, in letter after letter. The unity of the church across traditional lines of class, culture, ethnicity, gender, whatever: that, and only that, is the God-given sign that the new creation has been launched. Anything else looks like simply shuffling the cards of the old one.

Here, though, we face the huge question that returns throughout the book. For the Judeans, the Temple, as God's house, was the focus of *purity*. All impurity on the part of Judean people had to be purged away with sacrifice. All impure persons, such as the heretical Samaritans and the idolatrous Gentiles, had to be kept well away by strict rules. Hence the huge anxieties about Gentile inclusion.

Some preachers and teachers today might want to say, 'Ah, but, with the gospel, purity no longer matters. That's all mere moralism and we now know better.' But the story of Ananias and Sapphira shows that holiness, and the purity and danger that go with it, are still absolutely in play. So the sudden extension of the gospel to Samaria – and then to the Ethiopian eunuch – cannot be the result of people suddenly embracing a late-modern 'inclusivity' in which purity is no longer relevant. It can only be – as Peter says in chapter 15 – because God has 'purified their hearts by faith'. The gospel – and the new-Temple community – are not about abolishing the idea of the holy God dwelling in the midst, with all that that implies. They are about the gospel and the spirit transforming the impure so that they are impure no longer. We shall see in due course how that works out.

There then follows the strange case of Simon Magus. We needn't stay long on him here, except to note that his story in chapter 8 (verses 9–24) forms a kind of circle with Ananias and Sapphira in chapter 5. In both cases, satanic opposition tries to use money, whether to hoard it or to exploit it, to corrupt the pure witness. Money, like fire, is a good servant but a bad master. In those early days it could have set the whole thing ablaze. It still threatens that from time to time. We need discernment, utter transparency, clear speaking, decisive action. Wouldn't it be good if the Church could set an example to the world of how to do that?

But, underlying the story of Simon Magus, I note one thing in particular. In verse 11 we read that the people in that part of Samaria had been under Simon's spell for some time, since he dazzled them with some kind of magic. How easy it is for us to look down on the poor ignorant Samaritans, being taken in by a trickster. Alas, the history of the modern world – even the modern highly educated Western world – shows that people are still quite easily taken in by tricksters. Sometimes even by people, like Simon, who may have in some sense come to faith but whose hearts are still not straight with

God, as Peter declares in verse 21. We need to pray for discernment, in the Church and the world, recognising that whenever the gospel is going ahead, as clearly it was in Samaria, there are likely to be distortions and distractions which need to be confronted openly and boldly.

Chapter 8 ends on a happier note, with Philip's surprising spirit-led trip to the Gaza Road where he finds a pilgrim, heading home from Jerusalem, reading Isaiah 53 in his carriage. He asks Philip to explain it, and Philip is only too glad to do so. Luke has already hinted that Isaiah 53 was important in the early church's understanding of Jesus' death. Now, ironically, this is explained in detail, not to the proper teachers in Jerusalem but *to a Gentile, and a Gentile who as a eunuch could never have been acceptable as a proselyte, could never have been welcomed right into the Temple.* The new-Temple reality has reached out to Samaria. It is now reaching out to a Gentile eunuch, who is assured, when he believes, that he can be baptised at once and welcomed as a full member into the strange, newly sanctified, new-Temple family.

Part of the irony here is that, just three chapters after Isaiah 53, which the Ethiopian had been reading, there is the promise of a welcome to eunuchs (Isa 56:4–7). Perhaps, we may speculate, the man had been reading that passage, and had then been looking back at Isaiah 53 to see on what basis God could, after all, make possible his acceptance, his welcome. And it's in Isaiah 56:7, too, that the prophet declares that God's house is a house of prayer for all the nations – the passage Jesus quoted in Luke 19:46. Perhaps someone had mentioned that, too, to the Ethiopian. It all hangs together. Once again, Luke has emphasised that the Isaianic message about Jesus is the good news for which, whether it knew it or not, the world had been waiting.

Conclusion

Reading Acts 1 – 8 this way points forward to many later themes that might otherwise appear puzzling. Tensions continue over the Temple, and also over the church's view of official rulers, both Judean and Gentile. Jesus' followers, embodying with him the new heaven-plus-earth *reality*, are themselves equipped with a new kind of *authority*, cutting across existing authorities in a quite new way. They are sent out into the wider world to embody that reality and to exercise that authority – as, indeed, are Jesus' followers from that day to this.

As often happens, in Scripture and in real life, the next new stage begins, in chapter 9, with a most unlikely candidate. The young man Saul, who had assisted Stephen's murderers, will now have his own heaven-and-earth moment. Nothing in his life, or in the world, will ever be the same again.

4

Acts 9 – 12

Breaking through the Gentile Barrier

Introduction

Acts chapter 9 explodes into life with the risen and glorified Jesus appearing to Saul of Tarsus on the road to Damascus. It's one of the most famous scenes in the New Testament.

What precisely happened, and how we describe it, has been controversial. When people speak of Paul's 'conversion', they often imagine that Saul of Tarsus switched from a religion called 'Judaism' to a religion called 'Christianity'. But that's clearly wrong. Such entities simply didn't exist. Similarly, when someone in our modern world gets 'converted', that often means they move from having no religious faith suddenly to having one, so the word 'conversion' might imply that Saul of Tarsus had previously had a merely formal and outward faith and suddenly acquired an inward one.

All the signs are to the contrary. Saul had been a devout Judean with a heartfelt faith, loving Israel's God and his torah. Saul belonged to a movement which was determined precisely to bring Judean practice out of the formality of the Temple and into the home, the family, the street, into the heart and mind. No: something *happened* all right, something that turned Saul right around. But it wasn't what we often mean by 'conversion'.

So what was it, then? Acts and the letters make it clear that Saul/Paul saw Jesus. That doesn't mean that Paul's existing theology stayed intact, except for the fact that now he knew the name of the Messiah. Yes, he still worshipped the God of Abraham,

51

Isaac and Jacob, the God who made the world, the God who gave Israel the torah. But what happens to your vision of God when he sends his Messiah at last – and he gets crucified? That's the question. It sounds (and Saul must have seen it like this) like blasphemous nonsense, not just because crucifixion implied God's curse, but because the Messiah, as the true anointed king, sums up the life and fate of the nation in himself. Thus a crucified and risen Messiah means – if we can put it like this – a crucified and risen Israel. That is why Paul could later write, 'Through the law I died to the law, so that I might live to God. I have been crucified with the Messiah.'[1] As old Simeon had said in the Temple, 'This child has been placed here to make many in Israel fall and rise again.'[2] God's people were radically redefined around God's son. Paul never stopped worshipping the one God. But now he had seen into the heart of God's long-term plan in a way he'd never before imagined. Acts sketches that radical redefinition.

What really happened to Saul

So what really happened? Did Paul see Jesus with his own eyes, or was it – as many debunkers have suggested – an interior 'vision' without an objective correlate? Paul was clear in 1 Corinthians 15:3–11 that his 'seeing' of Jesus belonged in the same category as the other 'seeings' by Peter and the rest. At the same time, he distinguished his own experience of seeing Jesus from such visions and revelations as later believers might sometimes have.[3] When we read Acts 9 in the light of what we've seen in the book so far, this is another heaven-and-earth moment, puzzling to Epicureans ancient and modern (who believe that heaven and earth remain totally out

---

1   Galatians 2:19.

2   Luke 2:34.

3   1 Corinthians 9:1–2, where Paul's having 'seen' Jesus sets him apart from the Corinthian church, who had many spiritual experiences, including visions, but had not seen Jesus personally in the same way that Paul had. See *RSG*, ch. 8.

of reach to each other), nonsense to sceptics ancient and modern (who doubt whether there is a 'heavenly' world at all), but full of rich meaning for a Judean who believed that heaven and earth were meant to overlap, and that heaven itself now contained, and sometimes displayed, the now reigning Jesus.

Saul of Tarsus, as a devout Pharisee, is likely to have been praying as he travelled, as indeed one might, meditating on a psalm or whatever. A zealous Judean of Paul's day might well be contemplating Ezekiel chapter 1: the whirling wheels, the throne-chariot itself and the figure on the throne. There is a rich Judean tradition of such prayerful meditation. This is speculation: but it makes good sense to imagine Saul, jogging along on his horse or donkey in the midday heat, moving in devout contemplation from the wheels . . . to the throne . . . to the figure on the throne . . . and then, with a thunderous shock, seeing now not with his heart and imagination but with his real wide-awake eyes, seeing the face of the one on the throne, and realising that it was Jesus.

In that moment, everything he had ever hoped for, longed for, prayed for was fulfilled – and everything he had hoped, longed or prayed for was smashed to the ground. The hope of Israel had come to life, but in the most shocking way imaginable. His deadly earnest mission, as a zealous Pharisee seeking to purify Israel from blasphemous pollution, was turned inside out and upside down. He had himself been persecuting God's Messiah! – and now he was being commissioned, with a touch of dark divine humour, to go *as a zealous Judean* to announce the biblical good news to the Gentiles. Saul/Paul never doubted the God of Abraham, Isaac and Jacob. But he had to come to terms with the fact that he had radically misunderstood what Israel's God was doing, and hence also what, in the last analysis, he was really like.

When Saul arrives in Damascus (Acts 9:10–19) he remains stunned, and indeed blinded by the experience. But then we have another revelation, almost as remarkable. We are introduced to a disciple in Damascus named Ananias; and we watch as Jesus explains to this Ananias, in scriptural terms, that Saul is to carry Jesus' name before nations and kings, and the children of

Israel too.[4] Ananias offers us a quiet model of dangerous obedience. He goes, he greets Saul, Saul is able to see again, he is baptised, he takes some food. Saul's new vocation will haunt him all his life. Think again of Simeon in Luke 2: a light for the Gentiles, and glory for Israel.

Saul is told, more specifically, that he himself will face great and continual suffering. That indeed comes true almost immediately, as he begins to announce Jesus as Messiah in the Damascus synagogues, resulting in plots against his life, with himself being let down over the wall in a basket and running away. Galatians fills in some of the gaps in the story, but not all. Saul gets into trouble back in Jerusalem too: he is, it seems, far too articulate an evangelist and apologist for his own good. The Jerusalem believers pack him off back to Tarsus. There is almost an audible sigh of relief in Acts 9:31: he's gone, the church is now at peace. Saul was almost as much trouble when he was on your side as he was when he was against you. He would say boo to every goose in the yard, and then to all the swans as well. With Israel's Scriptures richly present to his mind, and the risen Jesus burningly alive in his heart, he wasn't going to mess around or tolerate sloppy thinking or half-baked arguments. Luke is preparing us for chapters 13 – 28, when all this is on continuous display.

We are not told, though, either by Paul or by Luke, what Saul did back home in Tarsus in the decade between the Jerusalem church sending him there and the time when Barnabas went to fetch him to help in Antioch (as we'll see at the end of chapter 11). I think it's fair to say that he prayed, and he argued, and he thought, and he wept – often all at the same time. And that he grieved over those of his family who would not accept what he told them about Israel's extraordinary Messiah.[5]

---

4   The scriptures in question would include Isaiah 52:13–15, and several passages in chs 60 – 62.

5   I have explored this further in *PB*, ch. 3.

God stops persecution

Let's step back from Saul's remarkable story for a moment and look at what happens when we take chapters 9 – 12 at a run. They start with a serious threat from a zealous Pharisee – and God rescues the church from the threat and turns the persecutor into a fearless in-your-face missionary. Skip across to chapter 12, which opens with the threat from King Herod Agrippa, trying to curry popularity with the Judean people, alarmed as they were at this new, subversive movement. He has James the brother of John killed, and he intends to kill Peter too. But again, God provides rescue. This time it comes, first, through another angelic jailbreak; and then, second, when God allows Herod Agrippa to overreach himself, playing at being a standard pagan monarch. Josephus tells us that, when addressing the people of Tyre and Sidon, Herod dressed in a splendid metallic robe that reflected the sun's rays . . . as though he was divine, a revelation from heaven. Herod in chapter 12 is a parody of the exalted Jesus in chapter 1. And immediately he is struck down by a nasty disease and dies.

The first half of Acts, then, sees Jesus exalted as the true King of the Judeans; and then look what happens to the present king of the Judeans. Yes, there is persecution. Yes, it can get very nasty. *But God . . .* in this case (12:24), 'But God's word grew and multiplied.' In Greek, *ho de logos tou theou ēuxanen kai eplēthyneto* – the same Greek roots as in the Septuagint of Genesis 1:28, commanding the image-bearing humans to 'be fruitful and multiply'. The renewed-human project is getting on track through the powerful creative Word of God. The true King of the Judeans is exalted; the fake one overreaches himself and comes to a bad end; and God's word is fruitful and multiplies. That's the outer frame of Acts 1 – 12.

While we're in chapter 12, let's notice a couple of details. On the night before Peter is to be killed as James had been, the church is praying fervently and the angel gets Peter out of jail. If I were the mother of James, I wouldn't like Acts 12. How come Peter got out and my boy didn't? I suspect the early Christians wouldn't have asked that question; they took random persecution for granted.

Presumably they had been praying for James as well, and Herod killed him anyway. Perhaps that's why, when Peter comes knocking on the door, they don't believe it's him. The maid Rhoda forgets in her excitement to let him in, but she insists that it is Peter's voice, and the response is, 'It must be his angel!'

That is a curious point in itself, worth stopping on for a moment. People in the ancient world knew (just as well as people today who've studied these things) that sometimes, when someone you know has died, they may appear to you – even if they've been many miles away – and then disappear again. We had an incident like that once in my wife's family. I have a friend whose daughter was killed in a random drive-by shooting, and the first indication the family had of the tragedy was that she appeared briefly to her fiancé, who was on the other side of the country at the time. Such strange things were and are well known. The way the ancient Judeans referred to them was to speak loosely of seeing someone's 'angel' or 'spirit'. So when Rhoda says she's heard Peter knocking on the door they think Peter has indeed been killed, like James, and that this is one of those post-mortem visitations. First-century folk knew perfectly well the difference between a vision and solid, this-worldly reality, as indeed in verse 9, where Peter thought his angelic visit was just a vision and then discovered it was real. The praying church thought Peter's voice was some kind of ghostly apparition, and then found it was real. These distinctions matter, not least because people today often glibly assume that people in the ancient world were gullible, and liable to confuse a vision with hard-edged reality.

So there, then, is the frame of these four chapters, 9 – 12. God stops the persecutors in their tracks. In the first case, he does it by converting Saul. In the second, he does it by rescuing Peter and judging Herod.

Peter and Cornelius: the Messiah as lord of the whole world

In between the frame of chapters 9 – 12, we focus mostly on Peter, starting with chapter 9:32. Peter heals a paralysed man in Lydda, west of Jerusalem. He is then summoned to Joppa, down on the coast, where a much-loved disciple, Tabitha, has just died. Peter raises her to life. Luke is establishing Peter's credentials as someone through whom God is doing remarkable work, preparing us for chapters 10 and 11, where Peter appears to go off piste theologically in a way that took Peter himself, never mind his friends back in Jerusalem, totally by surprise. If you're in ministry and you want God to do new things, get on prayerfully doing the present things and be ready for surprises.

Luke's account of Peter's visit to Cornelius suddenly goes into slow motion. First, Luke tells the story in chapter 10, then Peter repeats it at some length in 11:4–18 when he's quizzed by the suspicious group in Jerusalem. Even in the original telling, we have substantial repetition: Luke tells us about the angel visiting Cornelius in chapter 10:1–8, and then Cornelius himself tells the same story in verses 30–2. Why has Luke gone to such laborious lengths? Good writers – and Luke is one of the best writers among the early Christians – don't repeat themselves without very good reason.

The answer may be similar to the reason why Peter and John went to Samaria in chapter 8. It has to do with the perceptions of Paul and Peter in the early church, and the potential tensions surrounding Paul's thought-out policy of admitting believing Gentiles to the church without circumcision.

Much of the rest of Acts will be about Paul. We will watch as Paul goes on his missionary journeys, but then receives a hostile reception back in Jerusalem. Many at that time, including many Jesus-followers, went on believing that Paul was compromising Israel's holiness and purity by fraternising with Gentiles, telling them they needn't obey the law. We who live in a world full of conspiracy theories, rumours and scare stories need not be surprised that, when word went round that Paul was being a disloyal Judean, people believed it, magnified his supposed errors and were ready to use violence against him if they could.

But if much of Acts is about Paul, the only time after the present passage where Peter shows up is in chapter 15, where he supports Paul's non-requirement of circumcision for Gentile converts, referring back to this incident with Cornelius as the first time Gentiles came to faith. So in chapters 10 and 11, Luke seems to be making it laboriously clear, underlining it again and again, that the later Pauline mission to the Gentiles was not a dangerous break-away movement. It was fully in line with what Peter had already done. The modern version of the rumours that went round in Paul's day might be the idea, suggested by some influential scholars, of a 'Petrine' church representing something called 'Judean (or 'Jewish') Christianity' and a 'Pauline' one representing something called 'Gentile Christianity'.

Please note: that theory was deliberately privileging a viewpoint which could be claimed as 'Pauline' – and hence as Lutheran! – while being in fact a form of Enlightenment liberalism with a dark anti-Jewish edge. The theory emerged, in particular, from a version of the philosophy of Hegel, with 'Jewish Christianity' and 'Gentile Christianity' as the Hegelian 'thesis and antithesis', and then with the emerging so-called 'early catholic church' as the 'synthesis' that brought them together. That's what happens when you try to do history by starting with a philosophical theory and working down to what, according to the theory, 'must' have happened. You end up with what looks at first sight like a neat, clever developmental scheme . . . [6]

To reach that conclusion, however, you have to push some of the data off the table. That is why scholars who were thinking that way disliked Luke and Acts, because Luke specifically denies any such ecclesial bifurcation. Paul's Gentile mission was *not*, in fact, a separate movement which could be claimed as proto-Lutheran or anti-Jewish. There were never two things which could be called 'Judean (or Jewish) Christianity' and 'Gentile Christianity'. Jesus the crucified and risen Messiah, and the gift of God's spirit, take their meaning from the biblical world which always said that, when God fulfilled his promises to Israel, then Gentiles would come in too, not as a separate body. 'The princes of the peoples', declares the psalmist, 'gather as the people of the God of Abraham'.[7] There will

6 On all this see *HE*, esp. chs 1–4.

7 Psalm 47:9.

be one enlarged people of God, not two. There is at the moment a fad in Pauline studies for something that calls itself 'Paul within Judaism'. This movement suggests, absurdly, that at the beginning Christianity was for Gentiles while Judeans could stay as they were. But Paul's point always was that from within Judaism – from within the deepest truths of its Scriptures – there came Israel's Messiah, fulfilling the ancient hopes, even if not in the way people had expected. The 'Paul within Judaism' movement is in fact a way of avoiding the challenge of the gospel. Paul himself insisted that he *was* within the Judean world. That's why he went on going to the synagogue, even when they beat him and threw him out. That's why he went back in the end to Jerusalem, even though he knew it might cost him his life. So I'm suggesting that Luke has given us this slow-motion picture of Peter and Cornelius, not least to emphasise the underlying unity of the different branches of the early church.

So if that's what Luke is doing, how does it work in detail? The key is the parallel between the unclean animals in Peter's vision of the sheet let down from heaven and the supposedly unclean Gentiles knocking on the door downstairs. The two go closely together, as sociologists would insist: what you eat and who you eat it with belong together. The 'unclean foods' in Leviticus are symbolic warnings against intermingling with pagan idolaters.

The clue comes in the voice from heaven in Acts 10:15: *what God has made clean*. This does *not* mean 'what God mislabelled in Leviticus and now is relabelling'; but what really was unclean before is now, or is now being, made clean. I detect an echo here of Mark 7:19, where Mark interprets Jesus' words as indicating that all foods are now clean, which goes with what Paul says in Romans 14:14 about nothing being unclean in itself. But when it comes to fellowship with Gentiles, remember that when, in chapter 8, we saw the 'inclusion' of Samaritan believers and the Ethiopian eunuch, that didn't mean that the church had softened the need for purity, anticipating a late-modern shoulder-shrugging inclusivity. It meant, rather, that the gospel itself had done its cleansing, transforming work, *so that those Gentiles were unclean no longer*. The lesson Peter learned on the rooftop – and then had to apply to

Cornelius's messengers, and ultimately to Cornelius himself and his family – was that the gospel of Jesus does indeed cleanse idolaters, transforming them into worshippers of the one God we know in Jesus. That, too, is the point that Paul was making – to Peter, ironically! – in Galatians 2:15–21.

Now Cornelius was already a God-worshipper. Many Gentiles in the ancient world admired the Judean people for the purity of their monotheism and the accompanying purity of their ethic. Unlike Saul of Tarsus, who (in his own words) had had a zeal for God but not according to knowledge,[8] Cornelius, outside the Judean tradition, had been attracted by the Judean belief in the one God. He had found himself drawn in to be a man of prayer, worship and almsgiving: a knowledge of God, though without the Judean zeal.

So what does all that mean? Remember how we stressed earlier that the story of Samaritan converts wasn't a blueprint for modern 'second blessing' theology. In the same way, this story is not hinting at the post-Enlightenment idea that all religions are really the same, so that Cornelius is, or could be, a model for people in non-Christian cultures (like Mahatma Gandhi, say) who admire genuine Christianity, as it were acknowledging Jesus from afar. Those are our questions, not Luke's. Peter's message is precisely *not*, 'Well, Cornelius, you seem to be doing just fine as you are; don't let me impose on your present spirituality.' No: Cornelius needs to know about Jesus. That's why the angel told him to send for Peter. And when he *does* hear about Jesus, then the spirit descends.

So, just as Luke describes the violence and anger of many non-Christian Judeans, so here he highlights the generosity and eager devotion of this as yet non-Christian Gentile. We assume from the fact that Cornelius worships the one God that he has already thrown out his normal pagan idols. Non-Judean families would normally have many statues and small shrines dotted around the house or garden, as in a pagan city such statues and shrines would be placed at street corners as well as in official temples. So we assume that Cornelius has already got rid of his domestic gods.

---

8   Romans 10:2–3.

But he still has some way to go. When Peter arrives, he kneels down as though to worship him, and Peter has to tell him quickly to get up again.

Peter then summarises the Jesus-story in terms of the message of 'peace' (10:36) that Jesus brought. Interestingly, that is exactly the point, rooted in Isaiah, which Paul emphasises in Ephesians 2:11–22, precisely when speaking of God breaking down the Judean–Gentile barrier. So Peter then tells him the story of Jesus. Like the other summaries in Acts, we may assume Peter said quite a bit more than we have here, though this covers the bases: Jesus went around doing good and healing, including exorcisms. He was crucified – Peter doesn't say why, or attempt to interpret the event – but God raised him from the dead. There are two immediate results. First, Jesus has been appointed as the judge of the living and the dead. Second, Jesus is the one – as in the prophets – through whose name all believers receive forgiveness of sins. (We remind ourselves that 'forgiveness of sins', for a Judean of the time, had the larger overtones of God rescuing his people from the prolonged exile. For a Gentile it had the larger overtones of rescue from idolatry and its consequences, so that there was no longer any bar to being accepted in God's people.)

At this, the holy spirit falls on the assembled company, and Peter declares – like Philip with the Ethiopian eunuch – that they can and must be baptised. There is *no mention of circumcision*. That's the point. The Messiah is lord of the whole world. These Gentiles, believing in the Messiah, do not have to become Judeans in order to belong to his family.

Of course, back in Jerusalem, Peter finds himself grilled (11:2) by 'those who wanted to emphasize circumcision', *hoi ek peritomēs* in Greek, literally 'those of the circumcision'. This doesn't just mean 'those who happened to be circumcised' – Peter of course was himself circumcised – but his critics were 'those of the circumcision *party*', that is, believers who thought that, because the Jesus-movement was the fulfilment of Israel's Scriptures, Jesus-believers from outside Judaism would have to become full Judeans by getting circumcised. This controversy will return in chapter 15;

61

Luke emphasises here that Peter was the first to address it. Earlier in the book, we saw the apostles insisting that, if it comes to that, we must obey God rather than the authorities. Now we see a different point: that we must obey God rather than the pressure-groups. Both call, of course, for discernment, for sensing wisely when it's the moment to take a stand and risk disapproval.

Perhaps the most important thing in his explanation is the context of prayer. Cornelius was already a man of prayer, and his vision was God's answer. Peter was praying at the regular midday time and then *he* had *his* vision. The implication is that Peter, and indeed Cornelius, kept regular times of prayer every day, certainly morning, noon and night. Remember what the lord said to Ananias in chapter 9, telling him to go to Saul: *he is praying, and has seen a vision . . .* We will see the same again and again in this book.

Now of course: prayer remains a mystery. We don't understand why sometimes new things happen through prayer while often they seem not to. We don't understand why the church prayed for James and Herod still killed him, and the church prayed for Peter and he got out of jail free. But Jesus himself and the early Christians urge us to persevere in prayer; and you only tell someone to persevere if you know it will sometimes be hard. The battle is on. We won't see the whole picture; we have to hold our bit of the line.

Sometimes, indeed, prayer seems dark and almost without reward. I think of R. S. Thomas's poem 'Folk Tale', likening prayer to standing outside a house and trying to attract attention by flinging gravel at a high window. It seems futile, he says, and one might be tempted to give up were it not for the occasional twitch of a curtain.

Like much of Thomas, that's a bit bleak; but that is often how it seems. Many great women and men of prayer have reported such times, and have often concluded that God was withdrawing in order to woo them closer in. Anyway: no doubt Peter, and indeed Cornelius, had said their prayers over and over . . . and then suddenly, the breakthrough. God's fresh revelations appear out of the blue, but regularly that new light bursts in upon people who have long been praying in the dark. Think about it: nearly half a millennium separated the great prophecies of Isaiah and the rest from the promised return of YHWH to the Temple. Faithful Judeans waited and prayed through many false dawns, until finally Simeon and Anna recognised Israel's Messiah. There is a reason why, in many traditions, including mine, ministers and clergy say what we call the Daily Office. You never know what new purposes and possibilities are waiting in the wings. But if you step out of the great river of prayer you may just never see them.

Grace and radical newness

There remains one vital paragraph, at the end of chapter 11. Syrian Antioch, about 400 miles north of Jerusalem, was a big, bustling city on the trade routes, a melting pot of cultures, languages, ethnicities and religions. (This, by the way, is not the only Antioch we meet in Acts; there is Pisidian Antioch in chapter 13. Just as there were many cities called Alexandria because of Alexander the Great, and many called Caesarea because of you-know-who in Rome, so there were many called Antioch because of Antiochus Epiphanes, the Syrian megalomaniac of the second century BC.) Anyway: Syrian Antioch was where the dramatic conversion of Gentiles, which had happened during close-up and one-off encounters between Philip and the Ethiopian and then Peter and Cornelius, began to happen more widely. The Jesus-movement there had previously been confined to the synagogue communities, but now it spread across to Gentiles. The Judeans who had believed in Jesus and had found a new joy and hope in his presence and love couldn't resist telling their non-Judean friends and neighbours, and some of them came to believe in Jesus too.

This may seem obvious to us with long hindsight – not least when so many Christians in the world today are not Jewish, and have little contact with Jews. But for anyone living in that first-century world with its well-demarcated ethnic boundary lines, it is extraordinary to think that Israel's Messiah, instead of smashing the Gentiles with a rod of iron as indicated in Psalm 2, would be welcoming them into his family and revealing to them that his death and resurrection were the means of salvation for them too.

Anyway, word reached Jerusalem and – rather as with Peter and John going to Samaria – Barnabas came north to see what was happening. And (11:23), he 'saw the grace of God [and] was glad'. That's a great way of putting it: grace is something that you can *see* – presumably when you watch Judeans and Gentiles sharing in prayer, sharing in the Lord's Supper, sharing their whole lives as brothers and sisters. You can't fake that. It's grace made visible.

No doubt Barnabas knew about the Cornelius incident. But many in Jerusalem had remained very suspicious, perhaps prepared to allow for Cornelius as a one-off but hoping it wouldn't happen too often, disturbing the well-worn categories. Barnabas could see, though, that what was happening had gospel fingerprints all over it. He stayed to help. And then, as things developed, he realised they were going to need some more high-octane teaching and leadership. They needed someone who really knew the Scriptures; who really loved Jesus; who really knew how to explain things, both to followers of Jesus and to puzzled or suspicious outsiders. So . . . he went to Tarsus to find Saul. The ten dark years of Saul's life are over. He joins in the teaching, preaching and pastoral ministry of Antioch.

And, tellingly in verse 26, Antioch was where the disciples were first called *Christianoi*, Messiah-people: a new category, neither Judean nor Greek, slave nor free, no 'male and female'. We should remind ourselves that nothing like this had ever been known before. The movement needed a new name. And, since they were always talking about the anointed one, the *Christos*, that was the obvious starting point.

The radical newness of this community shows itself dramatically in verses 27–30, when a prophet warns of a coming famine. I was struck by this in the spring of 2020, early on in the time of the pandemic. Some people were saying at that moment that this was a divine punishment, or that it heralded the last days, or whatever. I got into trouble because I said it was primarily a call to lament. Well, the Antioch Christians, faced with the prophecy of the upcoming famine, didn't say, 'Oh dear, we must have sinned' or 'God is punishing those wicked pagans', or 'This means Jesus is about to return'. They said: who is going to be in serious need? What can we do to help? And – who shall we send? And the answer was: we will send money to the Jerusalem believers, living precariously in community and under threat of persecution. And Barnabas and Saul will take it to them.

We may not at once see how earth-shattering this is. The Judean world had often before seen itself, more or less, as an extended and mutually supportive family. But now here is a multi-ethnic community thinking that way about people 400 miles away, across huge barriers of ethnicity and also theology.

This little incident speaks volumes about early Christian ecclesiology. It's about extended family. That was without parallel in the ancient world. The closest you'd come would be, on the one hand, the network of Judean synagogues, all ultimately linked back to the Temple in Jerusalem; but they were specifically all Judean, whereas the churches were precisely of very mixed race. On the other hand, you could point to the networks of the Roman civil service, stretching from Spain in the west to Syria in the east, north up into Germany and Britain and south into North Africa. But they were specifically Roman bureaucrats, all male, all middle class, all free. The Christians, though, were not only of every race but of both sexes and of every social group, not least slaves. So the church was introducing a radically egalitarian community, transethnic, transnational, translocal. Its only common factor was loyalty to Jesus – but of course if it really is Jesus you're loyal to, and if someone else is also loyal to Jesus even if they are totally different from you in background, upbringing, social class, whatever – why then you and they are part of the same family. And the point of family in the ancient world was that you helped one another out. You shared. If Western Christians had paid attention, the modern self-serving ideologies of race, and the terrible deeds thereby legitimated, might have been avoided.

So when we get to chapter 13, and see the exciting new mission that is launched, perhaps we are not surprised that it features the same Barnabas and Saul who had just demonstrated the church's transcultural unity, joining together the radically new community in Antioch with the nervous, inward-looking, persecuted church in Jerusalem. Unity and mission are part of the same thing.

Conclusion

Thus Acts 1 – 12, which began with Jesus exalted and proclaimed as King of the Judeans, and powerful works done in his name, ends with the sudden demise of the present would-be king of the Judeans, and with the word of God growing and multiplying. And Acts 9 – 12, framed by God's dealing in very different ways with violent opposition to this new movement, contains the seeds from which the worldwide mission will now grow. The king of the Judeans, as Scripture always insisted, was to be proclaimed as the lord and Saviour of the world. No matter what the principalities and powers might do to try to stop it.

5
Acts 13 – 16

Converts and Controversy

Introduction

When we get to Acts 13, we have the sense of 'this is where the story really starts'. There's a good reason for this. Acts, as I said before, is not trying to give us a full 'early church history'. It is highly selective and has a particular focus, and a lot of that focus is on Paul. Paul has of course already featured in the story, but we have a sense that now at last we are approaching his real work. Luke is going to unveil the vocation that shaped Paul's energetic and dramatic work, the calling through which he in turn gave decisive shape to the life and thinking of the church as it spread across the Roman Empire.

Luke is not simply saying, 'This is what happened next.' Like many readers, I have often had the hunch that part of the point of Acts is to *explain* and even to *justify* the mission of Paul – not just what he did, and how he did it, but why; and also why, though he was constantly attacked and misunderstood, he was in fact in the right, not deserving of blame or punishment.

Throughout the story, Paul always seems to be in trouble, official or unofficial. Accusations come his way, often mutually incompatible but enough to gather a crowd, start a riot, get him beaten up or into jail . . . and then somehow he comes out the other side. Luke seems to be saying, 'Yes, there has been trouble; but look – one court after another, one magistrate after another, even King Herod Agrippa, have all said that the man is innocent.' So his message to the reader seems to be: can you not draw the same conclusion?

That is, of course, quite a hard case to make. If I had someone working with me who always seemed to be getting in trouble with the authorities, I might begin to suspect – as the Jerusalem church had long suspected – that the problem lay with the person concerned. But Luke insists again and again that it's the present world that's out of joint and under judgement, and that the reason Paul gets into trouble is because he's the one who's standing straight up, who's telling the truth.

A year or two ago, I was discussing my work on Acts with my friend Richard Hays, and he said that this point reminded him of a scene in *Perelandra*, one of C. S. Lewis's science-fiction novels, where the hero meets an angelic creature from a different planet.[1] The angel – Lewis calls it an 'Eldil' – appears as a shimmering beam of light, which at first seems to be slanting across the room. But, as you look at it, you realise that it is standing straight up in relation to its own true world. From that point of view, it is your room, your whole world, that is on a slant. Something of that sort is going on throughout Acts, and I think particularly in the work of Paul. He is telling the truth of God's real world. We shouldn't be surprised if it appears crooked, indeed dangerously so, to many of his audience.

There are different theories about what Luke was really trying to do. Some scholars think that Acts was written many decades after the event, with the aim of re-establishing Paul's reputation. Others, myself included, would put Acts much earlier, as a document preparing for Paul's trial. It tells Paul's story in order to explain that the trouble he incurred was the result of bona fide work, and that the authorities should let him pursue it peacefully. That makes a lot of historical sense.

Acts is therefore also saying to the Church: be prepared for this kind of mission. Yes, you may well be surrounded by misunderstanding, anger, mockery and perhaps violence. But you need to hold on, trust God and speak out the truth of the gospel. And Acts is also saying to the wider Greco-Roman world: yes, we are a new

---

1 The book is also sometimes called *Voyage to Venus*.

kind of society; we don't conform to some of your traditional ways; but this is because the one God who made the world has, through Jesus, launched the new way of being human. Indeed, this is the *true* way to be human.

There is therefore a sense in which Acts is offering a kind of 'natural theology', reaching its climax in chapter 17 in Athens. I hasten to add that this is not in line with the normal nineteenth-century 'natural theology', which kept the Bible and Jesus off stage and tried to 'prove' the truths of Christian faith without reference to them. That's not at all what Luke does, or what he suggests that Paul does. The point is that when the gospel message generates new communities, quite different from the communities in the pagan world and also transcending the community of Judean people organised around the law of Moses, the entire effect is to say to the world as a whole: look, a new way of being human! A way in which all can join; a way that anticipates the moment, long awaited in Israel's Scriptures, in which the Creator at last puts right everything that's wrong in the world.[2] By Jesus, says Paul in Pisidian Antioch, 'everyone who believes is set right in relation to all the things which the law of Moses could not put right'.[3] And then in Athens, '[God] has established a day on which he intends to call the world to account . . . by a man whom he has appointed.'[4] The essentially Judean message of judgement, of putting the world right at last, is fulfilled in a way the Judean world had not expected, and in a way which, as we shall see in Athens, transcends the greatest justice the pagan world could imagine.

Violence against Paul and Barnabas

So why, in Acts 13:45 and 50, did the local Judean groups react with violence, forcing Paul and Barnabas to leave and head east to Iconium?

---

2   On different types of 'natural theology', and my own approach, see *HE*.

3   Acts 13:38–9.

4   Acts 17:31.

And why were they similarly rejected in Iconium in 14:2, and then in Lystra in 14:19? Here we are on very much the same territory as Paul's letter to the Galatians. People have debated which Galatians Paul was writing to – was it the ethnic Galatians in the middle of Turkey or the Roman province of Galatia in southern Turkey? On the basis of the archaeological evidence in particular, I am with those who conclude that Galatians was written to the churches we meet in Acts 13 and 14, those of southern Turkey, part of the province to which the Romans had given the name 'Galatia'. And the problem Paul faces in those places (Antioch, Iconium, Lystra and Derbe) is, at its heart, the same problem he faces when he writes that letter.[5]

Now at this point we easily go wrong, not least because Luke emphasises in 13:42, 14:3 and 14:26 that the problem was Paul's message of *grace*. We all too readily misunderstand this in terms of much later debates, stemming from Augustine and then from Luther. We imagine that if there's a problem with 'grace' it's because humans are proud and arrogant and want to save themselves instead of relying on God to do it. So, in that theory, Paul was teaching 'grace', while the Judean communities believed in 'good works', and were therefore cross with him for apparently undermining their moral teaching. But that way of reading the whole situation, and Paul's response to it, barely scratches the surface of what's going on.

Remember what Luke said back in chapter 11:23 about Barnabas going to Syrian Antioch and 'seeing God's *grace*' in the multi-ethnic Christian community there. As in Ephesians 3, 'grace' is a short-hand not just for God's free love in the gospel, but for God's generous outreach to the pagans. This was not – though Paul's opponents never understood this – because pagan idolatry and sin didn't matter after all. It was because, through the death of Israel's Messiah, the idols had been defeated and sin had been dealt with. As a result, any pagan who was grasped by the gospel could be a full and forgiven member of God's family. That's what Paul – and Luke – meant by 'grace'. A new Jesus-based theological dispensation, now thrown open to the whole world.

---

5   See my commentary on *Galatians* (2021).

In all this, Luke is leading the eye up to chapter 15, where the challenge is posed not just from Judean unbelievers in the Diaspora but from the believing Judeans in Jerusalem itself. What on earth, they are wondering, is Paul doing fraternising with unclean pagans and telling them they don't have to get circumcised to belong to God's people? Luke, in presenting these controversies, is suggesting that these strange new communities of Jesus-followers, called into being by the message of the crucified and risen Messiah, now indwelt and guided by God's powerful spirit, producing healing and hope, are as it were self-authenticating. As Barnabas saw in Antioch, the shared worship of the one God and the common life of mutually supporting love, slicing across traditional social and cultural divisions, told its own story.

So the older view, imagining that Judean people were resenting 'grace' because they were proud self-help moralists, simply won't do. We need a far more holistic analysis. This is about what we call 'politics', not *instead of* theology but as its incarnation.

So is Acts 'political'? Absolutely. In Paul's world, the *polis*, the city, formed a tight social unit. We need to reflect on how that unit worked.

The official leaders and magistrates of any given community in the Greek and Roman worlds were regularly also priests in the local cults. This was appropriate, granted that most believed that cities had two sorts of inhabitants. There were the visible ones, in other words the humans who lived there at any given moment. Then there were the invisible inhabitants, including perhaps the ancestors, but certainly the gods – the big gods such as Zeus and his unruly family, and the local cults such as that of Athene in Athens and Artemis in Ephesus. And the magistrates, the priests, were responsible for keeping the peace with both sets of inhabitants. Citizens had to stay in line both with one another and with the gods. Order mattered: the social order of the human community on the one hand and the interactive order between the humans and the gods on the other.

Staying in line socially meant keeping to the given social order. There were men; and there were women. There were slaves; and there were free people. There were rich; and there were poor. There were aristocrats, the so-called well-born; and there were the ordinary people, with prosperous merchants at one end and destitute poor at the other. *And the communities of Jesus-followers cut right across those distinctions.* A new way of being human. Scandalous already.

Likewise, staying in line religiously meant knowing what the gods wanted. Every home, every street, the marketplace, the major public buildings, not just the temples – all would have shrines small or large, acknowledged daily and hourly, celebrated with major festivals, processions and, of course, sacrifices. And in Paul's world there was a new, young god on the block: Caesar and Rome. Stepping out of line with the regular gods was courting disaster – fire, famine, earthquake, whatever. The gods had their ways of letting a city or individual know they were displeased, especially if they were being ignored altogether. Stepping out of line with *Kyrios Caesar* was even more dangerous.

And the Jesus-followers had nothing to do with the gods. That's basic, as in 1 Thessalonians 1:9, where Paul declares, as something he and his hearers know and take for granted: 'You turned to God from idols, to serve a living and true God.' The Jesus-followers worshipped Israel's God, the Creator; they invoked Jesus as *Kyrios*, lord; they were initiated into his family through baptism in water; they met regularly to celebrate that lordship with a ritual meal. But there were no priests, no temples, no animal sacrifices. They didn't worship the other gods on the side. They didn't consult auspices or oracles. They didn't *look* like a 'religion' as people knew it. Many therefore assumed they must be atheists. They were seen as dangerous antisocial misfits.

Perhaps I should add that in all my years of growing up in various forms of Anglicanism, and in various types of evangelicalism, this point about the early Christians appearing as antisocial misfits was never mentioned, let alone explained. Nor were we ever taught about the serious problems that people in Paul's world faced if they wanted to stop worshipping idols. Perhaps there were sociocultural reasons for that as well.

All this needs to be kept in mind as we follow Paul in Acts 13 and 14, as he travels to Cyprus, to southern Turkey, back to Antioch and Jerusalem, and then in chapter 16 across into Europe. We'll come back to all that.

The other key thing to get straight from the start is that everywhere Paul went there was another group who didn't conform. They were the Judeans. The Judean position was already often awkward. If we don't understand how Paul's mission made it far more awkward still, we won't understand Acts or Galatians, let alone their meaning today.

In Paul's world, there were Judeans more or less everywhere, many of them well established socially. The exile in Babylon was only one way in which they had been dispersed; many of them had lived for centuries in other parts of the wider world. They tended to be good citizens; Jeremiah had told them, after all, to 'seek the welfare of the city' where they might find themselves.[6] But their co-operation with local societies stopped at the point of keeping the gods happy. That was a red line for them.

The Romans had discovered, at least as early as Julius Caesar a century before Paul's day, that you simply couldn't force Judeans to worship the gods. They would rather die. The Syrians had tried to crush them in the second century BC. It hadn't worked. So in the first century BC, Caesar, a pragmatist as well as a thug, had struck a deal with them. 'All right, you Judeans must pray *to* your god *for* Rome and its leaders, *for* your city and its well-being.' Fine, they could do that. Across the Roman Empire, local communities came to recognise, more or less, that this was the deal. Often, of course, local people resented it. If there was a flood or a famine or a military disaster or a plague, then those who hadn't been worshipping the local gods were obviously to blame; sometimes the finger – and more than the finger – was pointed at the Judeans. They were the ones letting the side down. That's why there were anti-Judean riots and pogroms in various places. But mostly Caesar's deal held.

---

6   Jeremiah 29:7.

Of course, pagans looked on in scorn at the Judean way of life. They regarded circumcision as a fetish. They saw Sabbath-keeping as just laziness. They assumed that abstaining from pork, which was the meat of the masses, was a kind of snobbery. And, in particular, they couldn't understand why the Judeans had such a strict ethic about family and sex. The pagans regularly got rid of unwanted infants, especially girls, 'exposing' them to be eaten by wild animals or taken as slaves by unscrupulous people. The Judeans didn't do this. Many pagan men regularly demanded that their women have abortions. The Judeans didn't. Most pagans, particularly men, found opportunities for sex all over the place. The Judeans, by and large, didn't. Why not? *Because the Judeans were creational monotheists, believing in the goodness of the created order, not least its male–female focus.* When Paul tells the Thessalonians to avoid the sexual immorality you find among those *who do not know God* it's clear that believing in the goodness of the Creator God and reflecting that goodness in family and sexual ethics go closely together.[7] God made the human body. Most Judeans of the time believed that one day he would raise it to new life in the end. Bodies therefore mattered quite a lot.

Some pagans respected the Judeans for all this. Some tried to join them, either as 'God-fearers' such as Cornelius, or even as full proselytes. But many pagans regarded the Judeans as a dangerous antisocial nuisance, even if officially they were in the clear, with permission from Rome itself to abstain from worshipping gods other than their own.

Only when we have all this firmly in mind can we understand why Paul and Barnabas were driven out of Pisidian Antioch, and then Iconium, and why Paul was stoned in Lystra. And only when we've seen *that* can we understand the controversy that led to the Jerusalem council in Acts 15. The letter to the Galatians belongs in the middle of all this. As I have argued in my commentary on Galatians, I believe that letter was written to these same cities in

---

7   1 Thessalonians 4:5.

southern Turkey, some time after Acts 13 and 14 but before the council in Acts 15.

The crunch is this. The reason for the trouble was that the early Christians *were claiming the Judean privilege, the exemption from pagan worship*. Paul regularly begins his work in the synagogues, telling the story of Jesus as the long fulfilment of Israel's larger story. That's not just 'helpful background' or 'proof from Scripture'. It is putting down a marker, just as Stephen had done in his speech in Acts 7 or as Paul does with the Abraham story in Galatians 3 and 4. The point is that the Jesus-followers are not a new movement, sprung from nowhere. They are claiming to be true children of Abraham, because they belong to Israel's Messiah. They are therefore claiming the same privilege that the Romans had given the Judeans, the right to abstain from worshipping the gods.

But this was bound to be confusing, to say the least. The new converts were not Judeans. All sorts of misunderstandings would arise.

Judeans and Gentiles

This setting, and only this setting, makes sense of what happens next. Why was there trouble, on the mission field and then in Jerusalem itself? And what does it mean for us?

It doesn't take much imagination to see the point. Everywhere, magistrates and aristocrats would suddenly discover a new group of people who, though not themselves Judeans, *were not worshipping the gods* and claiming that this was because they were following a Judean called Jesus. That's bad news. Bad things, the people would think, will happen to our city. So – bad things may happen to *you* in reverse: if you don't show up to the processions or the sacrifices in honour of Zeus or Caesar or anyone else, you might expect a brick through your window, or to be beaten up in the street, or to lose your job, or your customers. That's what you get for following Jesus. Don't say he didn't warn you.

But equally there's trouble coming the other way. People who heard and believed the message of Paul and Barnabas would claim that actually they *were* Judeans, sort of, just not in the normal way. Paul had told the great story: Abraham, the exodus, King David and on to Jesus. Jesus is the Messiah, the fulfilment of Israel's Scriptures. His resurrection fulfils the Davidic promises, as Paul insists in Pisidian Antioch (just as Peter had done on the day of Pentecost). To use today's jargon, God has done something truly apocalyptic, blasting through all expectations, fulfilling Israel's story by throwing it open to all believers from whatever background.[8] Followers of Jesus are thus the true monotheists, and *must not* join in the normal local religions. And we can imagine the (pagan) civic leaders going to the leaders of the Judean communities and saying, 'Who are these people?' To which the Judean leaders might well say, 'We've got no idea: those strange wandering preachers who came into town seem to have attracted a following. It's nothing to do with us.'

What would the civic leaders say to that? They might say, 'We don't understand you Judeans, but this seems to be your problem. You'd better sort it out, or our folk, who've always been suspicious of you, may just boil over.' Judean communities, then as now, knew that was always a danger. And the Judean leaders might well go to any local Judeans who had themselves believed the gospel and say, 'Look, for the sake of peace and quiet, get these strange new friends of yours circumcised so that we can say they're all bona fide Judeans. Or we're all in deep trouble.' That challenge explains why Galatians is what it is.

There's one more serious wrinkle, and it's vital for understanding Acts 15. Back in Jerusalem, many Judeans were chafing under the rough rule of Rome, praying for the day when God would deal with those pagans once and for all and at last fulfil his promise to rescue his people and enable them to keep torah perfectly. As we saw in Acts 5, there were different strands of Pharisaic orthodoxy. In particular, the hard-liners were insisting that zeal for torah meant not only personal holiness but, if necessary, revolutionary violence. And some were saying that, *until* all Israel kept torah properly,

---

8 On 'apocalyptic' see my *PRI*, Part 2, and *HE*, ch. 4.

this coming liberation, the kingdom of God, wouldn't happen. Then, with Judean pilgrims regularly visiting from the Diaspora, word would get out that a strange Judean called Paul was going around the Gentile world telling people that they could become sort-of Judeans but that *they didn't have to keep torah*. Indeed they must *not* get circumcised!

So what do the Jerusalemites think of that news? They think, 'This is exactly the kind of compromise that will delay God's victory over the dark powers! In the name of God and torah and Moses, this man must be stopped!' And the Jesus-followers in Jerusalem, themselves devout law-observers but under severe pressure, seem to think that way too. Which is why some of them then go to Antioch, as we see in Acts 15:1, and also in Galatians 2:11–14, to say that Gentile converts have to be circumcised or they can't be part of God's coming great deliverance. And this is the moment when some people from Jerusalem also go to Paul's newly founded churches in southern Turkey to tell them that Paul only gave them half the message, and that the other half is that *of course* their males should get circumcised. Welcome to the wonderful world of Galatians. Complicated, isn't it? Much more like real life than the old caricatures.

I realise that getting our heads around all this will make demands on readers today, used to the usual low-grade misrepresentations of some Christian teaching. But the pay-off is that it will make sense of Acts and Galatians in a way that nothing else can.

So what do we see in these chapters? Paul starts off in the synagogues. We follow him and Barnabas (and John Mark for the early bit, until he gets scared and runs back to Jerusalem). They go through Cyprus, Barnabas's home territory; a sensible start. Then they sail up to Turkey and head for Pisidian Antioch, which had been refounded as a Roman colony after the Roman civil wars. It was modelled on Rome, and was indeed known as 'New Rome'. It was focused on Caesar's glorious and peace-bringing rule (well, that's what they said). It was a thriving metropolis. And that's where Paul starts off, in Acts 13:16–41, announcing Jesus as lord of the world.

He tells the story of Israel from Abraham forwards, reaching its climax of course with the Messiah. His point is not just to give historical 'background', but to stake out the very specific claim that those who follow Messiah Jesus are true and valid heirs of the great scriptural story. But the gospel of the crucified Messiah is scandalous to most, not least because of its immediate implications: that with the Messiah's death for sinners, and his victory over the powers, the Gentiles who believe are welcomed into the family. As he says in 13:38–9, everyone who believes is set right in relation to all the things which the law of Moses couldn't put right. And that of course includes particularly the Gentiles.

So when Paul is thrown out of the synagogue he goes to the Gentiles themselves, quoting Isaiah 49, one of his favourite passages, highlighting the Servant as the light to the nations (Acts 13:47). When God does what he's promised, then the Gentiles will come in too, *not* – of course! – to *replace* the ancient people of Israel but to *enlarge* that family. This is what Israel's Scriptures themselves had always promised, particularly Genesis, the Psalms and Isaiah.

All this is too much for the anxious Judean population. They are, quite naturally, concerned for their own precarious position in the local society and culture. So they raise up persecution. Paul and Barnabas are driven out of town.

As this plays out in chapter 14, reaching Iconium and then Lystra, we have a microcosm of the parallel message which Paul and Barnabas announced to the pagans. As often, it begins (in 14:8) with a healing story, in this case of a man crippled from birth. The people of Lystra suppose that Paul and Barnabas are gods in human form. Their local culture had stories about just that sort of thing. So they try to come and offer the two apostles worship and sacrifice. This could be quite a funny scene, featuring a solemn procession with oxen and garlands and all. But of course, much like Peter telling Cornelius to stand up, Paul and Barnabas are horrified. They try (14:15–17) to explain the difference between pagan gods and the true God, the creator and provider of the whole world. The pagan gods are just homemade personifications of different parts of the good and sustaining world made by the real Creator God.

The Creator God himself, having long allowed people to drift along in their ways, is now acting more directly. That is the implication of what Paul says.

This little speech – presumably heavily abbreviated here – points on to what Paul will say in Athens in chapter 17. It remains the essentially *Judean* message of creational monotheism, now focused not just on Jesus (in whom the true God *had* indeed arrived in human form!) but on the summons to repent, to turn from false gods to the true one.

The pagans don't like this basically Judean message. The local gods will be angry if people don't worship them. Certainly, the neighbours will be suspicious. Bad things will happen. Paul is discovering in practice that the gospel is a scandal to Judeans and folly to Gentiles.

The controversy in Acts 15

All that is in the background of Acts 15, as Paul and Barnabas make their way back through the towns and eventually back to home base in Syrian Antioch. Acts 15 was a controversy waiting to happen.

There are two things to get clear from the start.

First, the controversy in Acts 15, in which Paul and Barnabas make their case against the suspicious group in Jerusalem, has nothing to do with the sixteenth-century stand-off between 'good works' and 'faith'. It isn't about comparing different types or patterns of 'religion' and showing that 'faith' is a better thing than 'works', or that it is somehow more acceptable to God. That was never the point.

Second, Acts 15 is not designed to serve, nor is it appropriate to make it serve, as a paradigm for ongoing church debates where the cautious conservatives always lose and the innovating radicals always win. It's been all too easy for those with radical proposals to cast their opponents as the legalistic Pharisees and themselves as the good, free-for-all Pauline libertarians. That's an offshoot of the first mistake. In some ways it is even more dangerous.

So what is Acts 15 all about?

It's all about the creation of the renewed, enlarged people of God, people of Abraham, people of Israel's Messiah. We need to be clear – as Paul is in Romans – that to say that Gentiles don't need to get circumcised is not a way of saying that the Mosaic law was a bad thing. In Jerusalem, Peter takes up the argument, looking back to the conversion of Cornelius and his household. God has given these believing Gentiles his spirit (verse 8); and he has cleansed their hearts by faith (verse 9). Paul and Barnabas then back this up with tales from their missionary journey. (I suspect that Barnabas had told Paul not to push his luck by trying to work through the entire argument of Galatians with the suspicious assembly.) But then James, Jesus' brother who was becoming the central figure in the Jerusalem church, roots it all in Scripture, in verses 13–21. And they reach at least a temporary agreement (verses 22–9).

What matters is that these surprising new communities, enlarged to include Gentiles who, though uncircumcised, are now baptised-and-believing, should stick close to basic monotheism and the ethic that goes with it: no idolatry, and no *porneia* either. That Greek word covers most of what we would call 'sexual immorality', including but going beyond the forms of misbehaviour that were often associated with pagan worship.

This is important in some of today's debates. Underneath the prohibition on idolatry and *porneia* is the strong positive valuation of the good creation, just as in the short speech in Lystra and the longer one coming up in Athens. The followers of Jesus are to be rock solid on creation. One of our problems today, I think, is that though Christians officially affirm God as Creator, in the first article of the creed, we tend to play it down. We often focus instead on salvation . . . though, if that then comes to mean being rescued *from* the world of creation, as many today seem to think, we are back with the second-century Gnostics, who elevated their own secret 'knowledge' above the truths of creation and new creation. That, indeed, is where much of today's culture is, both inside and outside the Church.

There follows one of the saddest passages in the New Testament: the row between Paul and Barnabas in 15:36–41. The argument focused on whether to take John Mark on the next mission trip. But I suspect that, behind that, there lay the Antioch stand-off in Galatians 2. Paul was now wary of trusting Peter's nephew John Mark. He knew, too, that Barnabas himself had wobbled at the vital point. It all comes out in a rush of hot temper and angry words. Luke makes no attempt to hush all this up. It must have been well known in the church.

I sometimes wonder whether this incident lies behind the strange moment in Acts 16:6–8, when Paul, Silas and Timothy seem to lose their sense of direction. The spirit won't let them preach either in Asia (western Turkey) or Bithynia (northern Turkey). There are many times in ministry when we hit puzzles like this. But in this case, it's as though they have had to cool their heels for a while, to spend more time in prayer, and to wait for God's moment. Then, suddenly, in 16:9, they are called across to Macedonia, in northern Greece. The two main churches there, Philippi and Thessalonica, were to remain Paul's favourites.

Paul and the authorities

And so we get to Philippi in Acts 16. There wasn't a synagogue there, but there was a place where Judeans met for prayer. That's where they went; and that's where Lydia, a wealthy independent businesswoman, was converted. Paul and his companions went to stay with her.

But then we watch Paul getting into trouble again. This time the issues are quite different from what he'd faced in Galatia.:18: he exorcises a slave-girl who has an irritating spirit of prophecy. Her owners realise that Paul has ruined their business: she can't tell people's fortunes any more. They know that Paul and his companions are Judeans . . . so, having had the Judean population in Galatia against him, and also the hard-liners in Jerusalem, Paul is now in trouble – for being a Judean and trying to force Judean customs on Greeks! Luke may perhaps hope we will smile at this, because of course that's exactly what Paul had *not* been doing in Galatia.

But for a pagan mob, always ready for a bit of Judean-bashing, it'll do. Verses 20–1: these men are Judeans, they say, 'and they are teaching customs which it's illegal for us Romans to accept or practice'.

These 'customs' may simply be the new practice of non-Judeans worshipping the God of Israel through the name of Jesus. Or they may be assuming that Paul is telling Gentiles to keep ordinary Judean customs. Paul doesn't have long to smile at the irony of being accused one minute of going soft on Judean customs and the next of advocating Judean customs illegally. He and Silas are beaten and thrown into prison.

The rest of the story is well known. Paul and Silas sing hymns at midnight, as you do. There's an earthquake. The jailer attempts suicide (because if the prisoners escape, he'll face torture and a nasty death). But Paul restrains him. He tells him about Jesus; he believes and is baptised; everybody is happy.

But then, in verses 35–40, we have a classic picture of Paul dealing with the authorities. 'Obeying God, not humans' also means 'reminding the human authorities of their job'. The magistrates send word to the jailer to let the men go. Paul keeps his cool. He's not going to slink away. He knows what happens to local authorities who mistreat a Roman citizen. And he knows that the local authorities will know. So, he says, 'Look here: Roman citizens! Beaten without trial! Imprisoned without charge! Sounds like a public apology.' And he gets it. And he deliberately takes his time about leaving town, stopping off to see Lydia and the other believers.

I bet Silas and Timothy were saying under their breath, 'Don't push your luck, Paul! Let's just get out of here.' But luck doesn't enter into it for Paul. The powers that be are ordained by God, and if they're not doing their job then God's people must remind them of it. This is by no means the last time we'll see Paul pulling off this trick.

This, too, is part of a kind of natural theology. God has ordered the world in a particular way. If it has been bent out of line, then part of the challenge of the gospel is to seek to put it straight. Paul believes that the God who made the world is in the business, through Jesus, of putting his world right. God wants advance signs

of that putting-right to happen, even in the present time. (That is
the mandate for all justice-work in the present time.) The church,
guided by the spirit, continues to have the responsibility to hold the
world to account, as Jesus said in John 16:8–10. Precisely because
we believe that God's putting-right of the world has been brought
forward into the present in the resurrection of Jesus, we are charged
with realising as far as possible – and circumstances will vary enormously on this one – the vocation to bring God's wise order even
into the present time. I fear that the Western churches since the
Enlightenment have barely begun to see how all that makes sense.

Conclusion

If it's early Christian natural theology we want, then the next chapter will show us what that might mean. We move on to southern
Greece. In Athens, and on trial before the highest court, Paul pro-
duces the speech of his life. And in Corinth, the local magistrate
gives a surprising verdict with surprising results.

6

Acts 17 – 20

Completing the Circle

Introduction

Acts 17 – 20 offers a multilayered tableau of Paul's work in the pagan world. We have Thessalonica and then Athens in 17, Corinth in 18, Ephesus and the riot in 19, and the speech to the Ephesian elders in 20. I am going to postpone the famous speech in Athens for the moment, because I want to devote a whole chapter to it, for reasons that will become apparent. There is so much material there that cries out for detailed study. Luke seems to me to have crafted his summary of what Paul said in Athens in such a way as to make it sum up a great deal of what it meant to be the apostle to the Gentiles: what happens when the very Judean message of the gospel of Jesus confronts the archetypal pagan culture and legal system of Greece? It's a Jerusalem-meets-Athens moment with a difference. So in this chapter we will put this to one side, pass over the famous speech, and return to it next time.

Throughout this section, Luke is setting out evidence for what Paul has been up to, why he was always in trouble, and how he was repeatedly acquitted or vindicated. This section, chapters 17 – 20, together with chapter 16 at which we glanced in our previous chapter, provides the central picture of 'Paul among the pagans'. These chapters raise *theological* issues about his central message and *political* issues as to why there were riots and opposition. They show clearly enough that theology and politics are bound to go closely together, not least if you're thinking as a creational monotheist.

Zeal in Thessalonica

Paul's short stay in Thessalonica (17:1–9) illuminates both questions. He and his companions do what they normally do, beginning in the synagogue and expounding the Scriptures, telling the great story of Israel, of Abraham's family and God's promises to him, then no doubt of David in particular, in relation to whom the resurrection promises stand out, as in chapters 2 and 13. This all constitutes (verse 3) the demonstration that God intended the Messiah to suffer and rise from the dead. We may assume that Isaiah 53 features prominently here. It all makes good sense. At least, a lot of local people think so.

But the Judean population as a whole are 'righteously indignant' (verse 5) – which Luke expresses with the word 'zeal'. (We recall that 'zeal' is a summing-up word for the whole programme of Pharisaic enthusiasm for the torah and the way of life that went with it, and in particular for the willingness to defend that way of life with violence where necessary.) This would not have taken Paul by surprise, of course. He had himself been a man of zeal, as he says in both Galatians and Philippians.[1]

Anyway, the zealous Judean population raise a crowd. Luke says they are a villainous lot, perhaps in order to deflect his readers away from any sense that the crowd had a point. They go hunting for Paul and Silas. (I assume Timothy was somewhere else. Perhaps Paul had taken care to shield the younger man from direct attack.) But, whereas in Philippi the accusation was that Paul and his friends were Judeans, teaching customs that Romans ought not to adopt, the Judean opponents in Thessalonica could hardly object to Judeans teaching Judean ways, so the charge is turned in a different direction. Paul and his friends, they say, are the people who already have a reputation for turning the world upside down. They are acting (they say) against the decrees of Caesar. It's not quite clear, at least not to me, what that might mean. But it *could* mean that, whereas Caesar had, broadly speaking, allowed Judeans to practise

---

1   Galatians 1:14; Philippians 3:6.

their own customs – including particularly their abstaining from the worship of pagan divinities – he had given no such permission to non-Judeans, and that Paul was trying to force open that door.

But the central charge, to which Luke builds up in a climax, is that Paul and Silas are declaring (verse 7) that there is 'another king, Jesus'! A *heteron basileia* in Greek; that's pretty explicit. This was bound to sound, and was intended to sound, like direct sedition and treason. It presumably stems from the Judean awareness about the meaning of messiahship. Paul's message about the long history of Israel reaching its climax in God's sending of his Messiah would have worldwide implications. In Scripture, the Messiah, if and when he were to show up, would be lord of the whole world.

The Judean community in Thessalonica were not about to say to puzzled pagans that this was of course built into their own Scriptures. Many Judeans of the time, like many Jews to this day, were content to regard the messianic prophecies in Scripture as a kind of allegory for a good time coming one day, which might well not pose a threat to the already existing authorities. After all, the Hebrew Scriptures ended with Cyrus the Persian giving instructions for the Jerusalem Temple to be rebuilt.2 Perhaps God would always be content to let the pagan rulers run the world, so long as they gave permission for the Judeans to practise their faith.

Well, perhaps. But Paul had never been that kind of Judean. Having met Jesus in person, he certainly wasn't going down that route now. Jesus was Messiah, therefore Jesus was the world's rightful *kyrios*, lord, a title claimed of course by Caesar.

Was Jesus then a king? Well, yes, indeed. Of course, some people in our own day, if accused of saying that there is 'another king, Jesus', might reply, 'Oh no, our message is purely spiritual.' Jesus himself did indeed redefine quite radically what kingship meant and ought to mean.[3] And to the charge that they were turning the world upside down, Jesus' followers would reply that they were in

---

2   2 Chronicles 36:22–3. In the Hebrew text, the books of Chronicles come last, after the Prophets and Psalms and other intermediate books.

3   E.g. Mark 10:35–45; John 18:33 – 19:12.

fact turning it the right way up. This was what the Creator God always intended: that his world should be ruled by wise humans, and ultimately by the Wise Human, the one Paul calls more than once the Image of God, the truly human one. So, however many redefinitions we may note, the central idea remains: Jesus is the true ruler of the world. When Paul speaks of Jesus' followers themselves 'reigning' as kings in Romans 5:17, he can hardly have supposed that Jesus was any less.[4]

Of course, this needs working out. Acts has a good deal to say about that. But this is the early Christian claim: Jesus is King and Saviour, and at his name every knee shall bow.[5] Any loyal Caesar-supporter was bound to see that as a challenge and threat.

So the local Judeans in Thessalonica manage, by dint of painting Paul as a seditious anti-Roman, to have him run out of town. He and Silas go on to Beroea, to the south. I'm inclined to think that, until then, Paul may have had in mind to continue heading west, along the Egnatian Way, one of the great Roman roads. That would have taken them straight to the port of Dyrrhachium, on the Adriatic, from where they could have sailed across to Italy and gone on to Rome. But perhaps that would be getting ahead of themselves. Perhaps, in the providence of God, the southern route was better, not simply to escape the pursuers from Thessalonica, but to face different levels of challenge in southern Greece.

Corinth: Jesus-followers as the true Shema-keepers

Not that they escape the pursuers that easily. They are followed to Beroea (17:13–14) and have to leave there quickly as well, though not before the more generous-spirited local Judeans give Paul and Silas a better hearing, and take the time to study the Scriptures in more detail. But the pursuers whip up a crowd there too, and Paul

---

4   See too Revelation 1:6; 5:10; 20:6.
5   See, obviously, Philippians 2:6–11; Revelation 11:15; 19:11–16.

is ushered away by sea to Athens. This, of course, forms a geo-graphic centre point for the book, poised as it were halfway between Jerusalem and Rome, and symbolising the Greek culture that, by Paul's day, had spread across the known world. We will follow Paul there in the next chapter, so that we can take more time over this Lukan centrepiece. But for the moment it's our turn to hurry on, south-west from Athens to the bustling seaport of Corinth. This takes us into Acts 18.

It's in Corinth that Luke tells us, perhaps to our surprise, that Paul was a tent-maker. Judean rabbis regularly followed a trade, and it's likely that this had been Paul's father's family business. This trade enables him, as it will here in Corinth, to earn his own living by hard physical work, so as not to be a burden on the church that forms around his preaching. And it's here that he meets, and stays and works with, Aquila and Prisca, who later he declares had risked their necks on his behalf.[6] It looks as though they were already believers. They had come from Rome after Claudius had expelled the Judeans, and perhaps they'd been converted through the early Petrine mission in Rome.[7] All that is another story. But it's good to remind ourselves of the physical circumstances of Paul's mission as well as of the implicit network of people taking the opportunity of the comparative peace of the early Roman Empire to be able to travel this way and that.

In Corinth, then, Paul follows the normal pattern: preach in the synagogue till they throw you out, then go to the Gentiles – in this case, right across the street to the house of a God-fearer who lived there. Luke emphasises that when Silas and Timothy finally catch up with Paul there, they find him full of energy in bearing forth-right witness to Jesus; in verse 5, Luke uses some words unusual for him, indicating that, for some reason, Silas and Timothy recognised

---

6 Romans 16:3–5; they are at the top of Paul's long list of people to greet at the end of his great letter.

7 The date of Claudius's edict is disputed (see the helpful discussion in Ben Witherington, *The Acts of the Apostles: A socio-rhetorical commentary* (Grand Rapids, MI: Eerdmans, 1998), pp. 539–44; so too is the question of the original foundation of the Roman church, on which see the very full study of Peter Lampe, *From Paul to Valentinus: Christians at Rome in the first two centuries* (London: T&T Clark, 2003).

that Paul was, as we might say, on top form. And at the moment, unlike in Thessalonica and Beroea, there is no riot brewing, perhaps because the ruler of the synagogue himself, obviously a person of some influence in the local Judean community, has become a believer (verse 8). Jesus then appears to Paul in a vision and tells him to carry on fearlessly. Nobody will be able to harm you here, he says, because he – Jesus – has many people there in Corinth.

The prediction that nobody would be able to harm him in Corinth forms quite a contrast with many other places. Paul must by now have come to expect trouble. But the prophecy would be fulfilled in an unexpected way, and with unanticipated results. Paul now faces a vital confrontation with the civic authorities.

Corinth was a Roman colony, with a proconsul as its governor. The proconsul at the time was Gallio, brother of Seneca, the famous philosopher who became Nero's tutor. We watch what happens in 18:12–17, remembering that in Philippi the *pagans* had accused Paul of being a *Judean* and *trying to teach Romans his Judean customs*. In Thessalonica, the Judeans accused him of seditious and treasonable teaching against Caesar and Rome. But this time, it's the Judean community hauling Paul into court with a very different charge. Verse 13: 'This man', they say, 'is teaching people to worship God in illegal ways.'

That is interesting indeed, and quite telling. The Judeans, we recall, were allowed by Roman law and custom to worship their God, and this regularly included the telling and retelling of their great scriptural narrative. So if Paul's message consists of the great Judean narrative, starting with Abraham and coming all the way up to the arrival of the Messiah, what's the problem? Don't the Judeans have official permission to tell their story in worship and thereby to praise their God? Well, say the Judeans, this man Paul is introducing other things which we disapprove of. They can't be truly Judean teachings. So Paul ought not to come under the normal Judean permission. So what were these things?

In verse 15, Gallio the proconsul declares that this is a dispute 'about words, names and laws within your own customs'. Words, names, laws and customs. I strongly suspect that this is a reference to the way in which Paul was praying, and teaching others to pray, the great Judean prayers – *but with the lord Jesus in the middle of them.*

I'm thinking of various passages. An obvious example might be Ephesians 1, which is a classic Judean recital of God's mighty acts, and which at every point includes Jesus the Messiah in the praise of what God has done and is doing. But I think here in particular of 1 Corinthians 8:6. There Paul, in the course of his argument about food offered to idols, effectively rewrites the daily Shema prayer, widely regarded as the very heart of torah. I strongly suspect that this reflects his regular teaching and practice.

The original prayer, taken from Deuteronomy 6, reads, 'Hear, O Israel, YHWH our God, YHWH is One.'[8] The Hebrew for 'Hear' is *Shema*; hence the name of the prayer. Now, in 1 Corinthians 8, Paul is actually discussing monotheism itself, not just referring to it in passing. He is teasing out the meaning of monotheism when it concerns food that's been offered to idols: if there is only one God, why might eating such food matter? Well, he says, we are of course monotheists, so we do indeed know that the great pagan gods are actually non-existent. There are indeed nasty little demons that will be coming at you, and that use pagan temples as their base, but there is no ultimate reality corresponding to the idols you find in those temples. 'Athene', 'Zeus' and the rest are figments of human imagination. Paul concedes that there are of course many 'gods' and many 'lords' out there in the world – he is probably including Caesar there – but for us, he says there is one God (the father, from whom are all things and we to him) and one lord (Jesus Messiah, through whom are all things and we through him). That rather dense English sentence corresponds to the original Greek; like many translators, I have added 'we live' to both halves of the formula, 'we live to him' and 'we live through him'.

In any case, the Greek here makes it very clear that he's quoting the Shema, and including Jesus in the middle of it. Jesus hasn't, as it were,

---

8   The Hebrew text can be translated in various ways; this rendering is one of the options given in the margin of the NRSVUE.

been added on to the outside of the one God. He is at the heart of the one God of Scripture and covenant. And Paul then goes on to expound this and to say, 'Well, if the crucified Jesus is central to who the one God really is, then his crucifixion must determine your behaviour, especially your consideration for the weaker brother or sister.'

Some of the synagogue members had come to believe in Jesus. But some of the other local Judeans then accuse Paul before Gallio. Luke doesn't spell out what precisely they say, but, if we work back from Gallio's response, we can get a good idea. Gallio declares that they are raising questions about 'words, names and laws within your own customs' (verse 15), and that he will not be a judge of such things, since they are internal to the Judean community. My guess is that the Judean accusers are saying (1) that Paul is using terms like *kyrios* (which in the Greek Bible was used for the divine name YHWH in the Hebrew) to refer to Jesus, (2) that his rewording of the prayer that summed up the biblical law was subverting that very law, (3) that the Romans had given permission for the Judeans to worship in their own way but that Paul was introducing a different way; and perhaps also (4) that, in using the word *kyrios* for Jesus, Paul may have been intending to substitute Jesus for Caesar himself. This makes good sense both of Gallio's curt response and of the larger picture of Paul's teaching and practice.

The point, then, is this. *Paul is claiming the high Judean ground: the followers and worshippers of Jesus are the real Shema-keepers, whether they're Judeans or Gentiles.* Jesus' followers are claiming to be true, authentic Judeans. And they can thus claim official permission to abstain from worshipping idols. The Judean charge is that Paul is corrupting the Judean teaching, and their practice of prayer, by introducing new 'words and names' to their central prayer, which in turn is central to their laws. Paul insists that he is well warranted in doing so.

And in Corinth, uniquely, Rome agrees. Gallio's verdict is that this is an intra-Judean matter, nothing to do with him. *In other words, Rome has declared, here in southern Greece, that the Jesus-movement really is part of the Judean world, and hence has official permission.* Paul would of course have carried on even without official permission. He did that in plenty of other places. That would no doubt have incurred persecution from all sides. But now he and the young church are in the clear.

So what's the result? No more persecution. Every other letter Paul wrote to churches involves mention of the recipients being persecuted. But neither 1 nor 2 Corinthians gives any such indication. Something is different here in Corinth. Rome has given permission. This, we think, is cause for celebration. The church flourished. Lots of people flooded into it. It became, in a measure, socially respectable . . .

And when we read Paul's two letters to Corinth, we see what then happened. The Corinthian Christians quickly became arrogant, puffed up, divided by personality cults, tolerating immorality, allowing nominal membership, taking a casual view of the sacraments, not caring about the poor, chaotic in worship. Soft on resurrection. Do you know any churches like that? Paul addresses those issues in his first letter. 'Do you think you've already become rich?' he says. 'I wish you really were already reigning, so that we could reign alongside you!'[9] They think they've got it made. Why should they pay attention to him?

His follow-up visit is then a disaster. Since *they* were in the clear, with nobody persecuting *them*, they looked down their noses at silly old Paul, always in trouble, always being beaten or shipwrecked or thrown into jail. He writes his second letter out of agony, personal and pastoral.

That second letter seems to have worked. But there's food for thought there for us today. How, on the one hand, do you stop non-Christian authorities from persecuting Christians? But how, on the other hand, do you prevent a church which isn't being persecuted from becoming lazy and arrogant?

Anyway, Paul's time in Corinth comes to an end (Acts 18:18). He goes back eastwards, and Luke gives us a quick summary of his trip: a quick stop in Ephesus, on to Jerusalem, up to Antioch, off again through southern Turkey . . .

Before leaving the Corinth area, Paul has his head shaved because he's under a vow. Luke doesn't explain this, but he leaves

---

9   1 Corinthians 4:8.

the impression that Paul is making sure to do what he says in 1 Corinthians 9:20: 'to the Judeans I became as a Judean' (my translation). Perhaps he did this in anticipation of going to synagogues in other cities, perhaps prior to the visit to Jerusalem. Perhaps he was keen to demonstrate his loyalty to Israel's ancestral traditions, as he would insist at various subsequent points. Anyway, in chapter 19, he comes back to Ephesus again, before which Apollos, a powerful speaker but originally only knowing John's baptism, has been in Ephesus and gone on to Corinth. Luke draws a veil over the implied stand-off between Paul and Apollos, which we detect behind 1 Corinthians. Luke doesn't encourage us to think in terms of people being totally good or totally bad, cardboard cut-out heroes or villains. As with the row between Paul and Barnabas, there may well have been right on both sides.

Turnaround in Ephesus

In Ephesus, Paul has a strange encounter with some followers of John the Baptist (19:1–7). This meeting, along with the remark about Apollos, reminds us that there were all sorts of things going on in the early church of which we know very little. Any attempt to tidy things up (or to make them fit modern developmental schemes!) is likely to be unhistorical. True history is full of all kinds of things that don't fit our tidy patterns.

Anyway, in Ephesus, Paul follows his normal practice (19:8–10): to the Judean first and also to the Greek. Synagogue preaching till he's thrown out, then public lectures in a rented hall. It is massively successful. Everybody in the whole region hears about Jesus. Ephesus was a major centre of magic and spiritual power. Paul gets a reputation for being himself a man of spiritual power. Healings were performed through handkerchiefs that had touched his body. Exorcists who tried to invoke his name came to a bad end (19:11–17).

The result, remarkably, was a major turnaround in Ephesus. A large number of magicians burned their books. Paul must have thought the gospel had won. Things had not just gone a bit better in

Ephesus than elsewhere. They had been massively successful. So, says Luke (19:20), the word of God grew mightily and prevailed.

But the dark powers have ways of striking back; and when they do, they don't play fair. Remind yourself of this, any pastors reading this, when your church or your youth group is overflowing and people say how wonderfully well the parish is doing, and when people greet you in the street and want to be your friend. You never know what's round the corner.

Luke draws a discreet veil over what happened next. Paul lifts that veil just a bit when he writes his second letter to Corinth. 'We don't want to keep you in the dark', he says in 2 Corinthians 1:8–9, 'about the suffering we went through in Asia . . . it got to the point where we gave up on life itself.' (Ephesus was the principal city of the Roman province of 'Asia', the western part of modern Turkey.) Luke doesn't tell us what had actually happened to make Paul of all people say something like that. What he tells us about is the famous riot. I suspect this was not unconnected to a serious time of imprisonment where Paul's spirits sank lower than at any other point of which we know. But of this Acts itself tells us nothing.

The set-up for the riot is similar to the situation in Philippi, though on a larger scale. In chapter 19:23–7 it emerges that Paul's ministry is bad for business. In Philippi, this was because he exorcised a girl who could foretell the future. In Ephesus, it was because his critique of idols – a regular Judean theme, now reinforced by the victory of Jesus – had been undermining the demand for domestic-scale statuettes of the local goddess Artemis. (You can still buy them there, by the way; there is a brisk tourist trade, perhaps less now for worship and more for souvenirs, though some might see the two as uncomfortably close.) Anyway, as far as the local craftsmen were concerned, the reduction in business was clearly a blasphemous insult to their goddess. Artemis (Diana in Roman thought) had her great temple in Ephesus. It was one of the seven wonders of the ancient world, *four times* larger than the Parthenon, Athene's home in Athens. So what we have here is civic pride melded with religious fervour. That's a toxic mixture, one with which today's world is, shall we say, not unfamiliar.

The chant from the crowd was the kind of thing you hear from angry mobs in parts of the Middle East today. 'Great is Ephesian Artemis!' It works much better in Greek: *Megalē hē Artemis Ephesiōn! Megalē hē Artemis Ephesiōn!* Paul can hear it, on and on, from his lodgings. He wants to go and address the crowd. Of course he does: he's Paul. But his friends won't let him. And some of the local officials who are friendly to him – obviously he's become a well-known figure in town – send him a message urging him not to go to the theatre where it's all happening.

Then, as elsewhere, things take a darker turn. Verse 33: a Judean leader called Alexander tries to speak. He probably wants to explain that Paul doesn't represent the local Judean community. As in other cities, the relationship between Judeans who had accepted Jesus as Messiah and Judeans who hadn't was bound to be fraught, and the Judean communities would quite naturally be anxious in case the Jesus-movement not only gained equal permission with theirs – the permission to practise their faith and not to worship the gods – but might actually upstage them.

But the fact that Alexander is a Judean only makes it worse. Everybody knew that the Judeans were opposed to idols just as much as Paul was. Indeed, this was one of the most obvious points of identity between ordinary Judeans and the Jesus-followers. So as far as the crowd were concerned it all came to the same thing.

Here is yet another irony. In Corinth, the fact that the Roman official declared that the Christians and the Judeans were all part of the same kind of thing meant that all was well, and both could practise in peace. In Ephesus, the same evidence – Christians and Judeans on the same page – meant that both were in danger.

But then the town clerk (a leading magistrate) tells the crowd to calm down. Rome had strict laws about riots, and indeed about unofficial gatherings of more than quite a small number of people. The whole city might well have faced a punitive fine, or had their much-prized civic status downgraded. So once again Luke is saying, 'Yes, there was trouble, but the proper officials came through on the right side.'

There are patterns emerging to all this, and it's worth pausing a moment to see how they play out, with their variations. In Philippi, the magistrates have to come and give Paul a public apology. In Athens (as we'll see in the next, specially focused, chapter) the members of the high court of the Areopagus laugh at Paul, but he gets off what had been a potentially dangerous charge. In Corinth, Gallio declares that Christianity is a variation of Judaism and therefore now has legal standing. In Ephesus, the town clerk tells the mob there had been no reason to riot. Different routes to the same result – and all pointing forward, as far as Luke is concerned, to the trial in Rome, which remains just out of sight after the end of the book. Surely, if all these magistrates do the right thing, then Caesar himself will follow suit when it comes before him?

But notice the variegated pattern, too, of the accusations in these chapters. In Philippi, Paul ruins the business of the slave-owners, and he's then accused of being a Judean and inculcating anti-Roman customs. An economic charge running into religious prejudice, and then civic sedition! In Athens, as we'll see, he's importing foreign divinities. In Corinth, he's teaching un-Judean worship, and so ought not to be given the official Roman permission. In Ephesus, he's undermining the trade in idols, as you'd expect from a Judean.

All in all, it's as though everybody is looking at Paul's gospel ministry and seeing something they don't like. The truth is in there somewhere, and people don't want it. Folly to Gentiles, scandalous to Judeans. A new community, quite unlike anything ever seen in the world before, breaking the social customs, challenging the political systems, inculcating a new type of worship. Bringing together in a single equal family slave and free, Judean and Gentile, female and male. No wonder Paul ended up with riots, beatings, accusations and goodness knows what else – as in the catalogue of suffering in 2 Corinthians. That's what you get for preaching the grace of God through the crucified and risen Messiah.

Hurrying to Jerusalem for Pentecost

So Paul leaves town and, at the start of chapter 20, heads round through Macedonia to Corinth and back again, via Troas where he lectures all night and poor Eutychus falls out of a window. (I have heard people say that Paul could preach people to death, citing this passage; well, fair enough: that's the risk you take if you go on till past midnight in a hot upstairs room.) Paul was hurrying (as he says in verse 16) to be in Jerusalem for Pentecost.

Why? Perhaps he was hoping to be able to address a large pilgrim audience. But, granted what had just happened – both what Luke tells us and what he doesn't! – that urgency for a particular occasion and audience in Jerusalem is probably not the only reason Paul doesn't want to go back to Ephesus itself. I sense him shuddering at the thought, as in 2 Corinthians 1. So he summons the elders of the Ephesian church to meet him in Miletus, a bit further south, just down the coast.

In the speech that follows (Acts 20:18–35), Luke seems to be drawing a line under Paul's travels in Turkey and Greece. Through his highlighting of this address, he is explaining Paul's work to puzzled or potentially hostile readers.

After all, the Mediterranean world of the first century was full of wandering teachers with dubious motives and practices. Philosophers both serious and trivial came and went. Many were out for a quick payment from a gullible audience, and would leave town before their hearers realised they'd been duped. Equally, as we know ourselves, many had darker motives again, seeking to lure impressionable people of either sex into a web of deceit and corruption. Faced with all that, and aware that anybody in Rome reading his book might well wonder about Paul's motives, Luke here emphasisesPaul's absolute integrity. Any of us called to ministry of whatever sort will do well to ponder this speech carefully.

Luke records it as part of his apologia for Paul. But why does Paul say it to the Ephesian elders? Partly because a message to Ephesus, the local capital, will travel throughout the region. But also because he knows from bitter experience that people will try to trash his reputation and accuse him of arrogance or greed. So, in verses 18 and onwards, he insists on the opposite. He has constantly told them the uncomfortable truths, the whole thing (verse 27). He hasn't been flattering them or currying favour. And they know that he wasn't trying to get rich on the side.

More specifically, in verses 19–21, he emphasises his own humility and suffering. In the ancient world, there was no private life, except for the very rich; the Ephesians would know well that Paul had indeed suffered a lot, often being reduced to tears. But in the midst of that, as in verse 20, he had persisted in preaching and teaching everything they needed to know. The picture of him in verse 20, going from house to house, is quite striking: like the old-fashioned clergy in my tradition, back in the time of seventeenth-century characters such as George Herbert or Richard Baxter, Paul was able to go through the streets seeking out members of his flock, to sit down and pray with them, weep with them, warn them, encourage them, challenge them. And the heart of it was always the new way of life, the Jesus-way: as in verse 21, this focuses on repentance towards God and faith in the lord Jesus. It means, in other words, what Paul said in 1 Thessalonians and elsewhere: *turning away* from idols and *turning to* the living God, and knowing the living God in and through Jesus himself.

But then Paul looks to the future (verses 22–4). He has his eye on the prize, as he says in Philippians 3 (perhaps written not long before this): forgetting what lies behind, and straining forward for what lies ahead. He knows – because the holy spirit has been making him aware of it – that wherever he goes, trouble is lying in wait. It doesn't take Paul a huge amount of spiritual insight to work that one out, granted what he has been through already. But as far as he's concerned, his life has only one purpose, 'to bear witness to the gospel of God's grace' (verse 24).

That blessed word again: *grace*. The biblical message of the God who wants, longs, to come and dwell with his people, and does everything that love can do to make it possible. Paul's message was always (verse 24 and again in 32) the good news of God's grace. As in Ephesians itself, and as earlier in Acts, the 'word of his grace' is shorthand for God's love reaching out to the morally undeserving and hence also the love of Israel's God reaching out to the Gentiles. The gospel of grace humbles all human pride; it humbles the Gentiles – fancy having to abandon their cultural history and worship Israel's God! – and it humbles the Judean people too. Paul has preached and lived this unflattering, humiliating, but life-giving message.

Then the bad news: he won't be back in these parts again, he says (how did he know that? Perhaps because he knew his vocation was taking him further west, to Rome and beyond). So, if it's time to say goodbye, Paul will do what other Judean writers and speakers had done: declare that, having fulfilled his own obligations, he isn't responsible for the blood of any of them. He is standing in a line going back at least to Ezekiel 33: he has been faithful to his prophetic call.

So he addresses the leaders with a severe warning (verses 28–31), which Christian leaders in every generation should read with fear and trembling. He echoes Ezekiel 34, the denunciation of shepherds who have been feeding themselves rather than the flock. Yes, he says, there will be savage wolves, including some from among you, who will distort the truth to draw disciples away. No doubt the wolves would say that Paul had got some things wrong and that they needed to put them straight. But Paul's ministry was validated (verses 32–5) by the life everybody knew he led. There is a word for us all. What mattered was helping the weak, in line with an otherwise unrecorded word of Jesus (verse 35) about 'giving' being more blessed than 'receiving'.

Conclusion

Paul's model of gospel ministry remains costly. The spirit (verse 23) is now telling Paul that wherever he goes he faces imprisonment and persecution, not least in Jerusalem. That will take us to our subsequent chapters. But first we must retrace our steps to Athens, and ponder the remarkable address that Paul gave in the historic high court of the Areopagus. Luke seems to have highlighted this, standing as it does near the heart of his remarkable book. It deserves a chapter to itself.

7
Acts 17:16–34

The Unknown God?

Introduction

Up to this point, we've been taking Acts in a few flying leaps. After
the introduction, we worked through chapters 2 – 4, 5 – 8, 9 – 12
and then at speed through 13 – 16 and through much of 17 – 20.
But, as I explained in the preface, I want deliberately to slow down
at this point and look in more detail at Acts 17:16–34. This is the celebrated speech that Paul made before the Court of the Areopagus
in Athens.

Some misconceptions

Paul's 'Areopagus address' is one of the most famous set pieces in
Acts and indeed in the whole New Testament. Luke seems to intend
it to stand here at the heart of Paul's mission to the non-Judean
world. There is what looks like a short version of it in chapter 14
in Lystra. But more generally, when Paul describes himself in his
letters as 'the apostle to the Gentiles', he must be envisaging this
kind of address. The speech is thus well worth taking time over,
both because Luke seems to intend it to be central and because of its
unique content.

We have to assume that Luke has given us a summary. You can
read the speech out loud in Greek in under three minutes. Granted
everything we know of Paul, there is no way that, if he was asked to

address the high court in Athens, he would keep it that short! But Luke, in boiling his speech down to basics, hasn't spoilt its balance.

The speech has been endlessly studied, not least by theologians who have discussed what at first sight appear to be Paul's attempts to find 'points of contact' with the pagan non-Judean world, shared assumptions on which he could build a gospel presentation. Paul, after all, has often been seen as the 'Protestant' apostle, saying 'no' to everything remotely pagan and wanting simply to give a message of salvation through the cross of Jesus. But here he seems to be affirming pagan symbols and quoting pagan poets and philosophers, and when he does get round to Jesus he speaks not of the cross, but only of the resurrection. Some have therefore concluded that this speech represents something Luke wants to do or say, but without much historical reference to Paul himself. The speech has often been seen, instead, as an essay in 'natural theology', in which one might begin with symbols in the culture, rather than with Scripture or with Jesus, and try to fit the gospel into the culture rather than having it address the culture with a fresh gospel-oriented word. That has been contentious, partly because it's not at all clear that that is in fact what Paul is doing here, and partly because that approach to theology is itself highly controversial. Another suggestion has then emerged, alongside the proposal that the speech represents Luke, not Paul: it is sometimes argued that perhaps Paul did indeed try 'natural theology' and the resurrection in Athens – and it obviously didn't work, so when he went to Corinth he took a radically different line. As he says in 1 Corinthians 2, he there determined 'to know nothing in my dealings with you except Jesus the Messiah, especially his crucifixion'.[1] Thus (so runs this argument) Paul leaves Athens quickly, with hardly any converts, but he stays in Corinth much longer, establishing a thriving church.

Let's just knock that last suggestion on the head before we move on. When Paul actually summarises his gospel, in 1 Corinthians 15, he stresses the *whole* Jesus-story: the Messiah, his death, his burial and particularly his resurrection. There's no either/or between

---

1   1 Corinthians 2:2.

Calvary and Easter, either evangelistically or theologically. And we must note, as we saw earlier, that a good deal of Acts, including the important early speeches, likewise focuses on the resurrection, with only brief statements about the cross. So this address isn't actually out of line, in that respect at least.

One more serious misconception to put aside as we begin. Many people have supposed that the Areopagus was a kind of philosophical debating society. Luke has just mentioned in verse 18 that Paul had been arguing with the Stoics and Epicureans. It's been assumed that this address is Paul's attempt to put his own position in that debate. Well, there are indeed philosophical arguments going to and fro here, as we shall see. But the Areopagus was not a debating society. It was a law-court: the highest court in Athens, composed of leading citizens, founded jointly (according to the local legend) by the god Apollo and by Athens's own tutelary deity, the goddess Athene. The name 'Areopagus' means 'Hill' or 'Rock' of Ares, Ares being the Greek version of Mars, the Roman god of war: hence the frequent translation 'Mars Hill'. The craggy hill in question is a mile or so to the west of the Acropolis, the larger hill in the city centre on which to this day you see Athene's great temple, the Parthenon, and sundry other temples and buildings. There are debates as to whether, in Paul's day, the court actually met on that hill or somewhere closer to the middle of the town. But the point is that it was indeed a *court*, not a discussion group.

The court in question, the Areopagus, had been set up initially to try the most serious cases, including capital ones. Its first defendant was the legendary Orestes, on trial for avenging his father Agamemnon by killing his mother Clytemnestra. The point here, anyway, is that Paul is being put on trial. When, in verse 19, Luke says they 'took him' up to the Areopagus, the word *epilambano* means to 'seize' or 'arrest'. It certainly wasn't about Paul being invited to give a learned paper at next week's seminar.

So why the fuss? What is the charge, and how does it relate to the charges levelled at Paul in Philippi and Thessalonica, and later in Corinth and Ephesus? In verse 18, we hear the reaction of the Athenians to what Paul has been saying in the marketplace: he seems to be preaching 'foreign divinities'.

At one level, this seems trivial. They heard him banging on about 'Jesus and Anastasis', and they imagined that *anastasis*, 'resurrection', might be a new goddess, perhaps Jesus' spouse. Well, Paul sorts that one out eventually. But the point – as we saw earlier – was that ancient towns and cities, though playing host to many gods and goddesses, distrusted the import of 'foreign gods'. That might mean political subversion, bringing in a new divinity who might try to take over, undermining the social fabric with its tightly woven religious elements. Remember the shout in Thessalonica that Paul and Silas were turning the world upside down, teaching Judean customs, and claiming that there was another king, namely Jesus. Think ahead to Ephesus where the focus of the riot is that Paul and his friends are proving a threat to the goddess Artemis. And, with dark irony, when he gets back to Jerusalem he's accused of polluting the Temple there. We're picking up a regular theme.

Back to Athens. The city's most famous trial was that of Socrates in 399 BC. He was charged with 'impiety' and 'corrupting the young'. The chief evidence offered against him was that he didn't acknowledge the city's official gods, and also – here it is – that *he was introducing new divinities*. Time for the hemlock, Socrates.

So we must read verse 19 differently. It isn't an innocent enquiry, with the officials merely asking, 'Can you please explain what you're talking about?' It's a suspicious, perhaps sneering, half-accusation: 'Are we *able to know* what this new teaching really is that you are talking about?' The Greek here hints that Paul might have been introducing a new mystery religion, which only the initiates could grasp. Exactly the kind of thing that might arouse the suspicions of civic leaders. People meeting behind closed doors, sharing dark secrets. Learning to dance to a different drummer. Very bad for social morale, that kind of thing. Granted, Luke suggests in verse 21 that the Athenians were simply out for novelty. But that looks to me like a way of scaling down the seriousness of what was going on. Luke can't disguise the fact that Paul gets into trouble wherever he goes.

But at least, instead of setting the mob on Paul, or staging a riot, his accusers here do the decent Athenian thing and bring him to a proper court.

The charge of 'foreign divinities'

So what is Paul doing in this dense and fascinating speech? Here we have to avoid bringing in the categories of fairly modern debate – just as we had to beware of reading Acts 2 in terms of the questions raised in Pentecostal teaching about 'second blessings' and the like. Yes, we can say if we want that he is beginning by referring to the local culture, starting with the altar to the unknown god, and (in verse 28) quoting Aratus, one of their own poets from 300 years earlier. Maybe, like many Judean thinkers, Paul could see that pagan culture did sometimes come close to the truth of God and his creation, even if it then usually distorted it. After all, Paul was a creational monotheist. As Psalm 19 indicated, anyone living in the created world was bound to catch at least some glimpses of the Creator's mind behind his handiwork.

But Paul is also *confronting* the local culture. In a big way. The true God, he says, doesn't live in handmade temples ('made by hands' was the regular Judean phrase to sneer at pagan idols). Nor does the true God, as Creator of all, need animal sacrifices. Now it's one thing to say this when you're sitting in a seminar room, or in a synagogue with Judean friends. It's quite another to say it on Mars Hill (or indeed almost anywhere else in central Athens), in full view of the Acropolis with its great temples – the Parthenon, the Temple of Nike and so on. You can see these stunning works of ancient architecture, these architectural statements of local theology and religious practice, from both Mars Hill and the marketplace. As Paul was speaking, there might well have been a procession going by, with singing and dancing, on its way to offer sacrifice. And Paul just waves his hand at these amazing examples of Athenian high culture and declares that they're a category mistake. They're a waste of space. This is hardly playing 'nice' to the local sensibilities. I said, from the start of Acts, that most of the pressure points would have to do with temples. Here we are again.

So the question of 'Paul and culture' can go both ways. That suggests that it's the wrong question, interesting though it is in its way. This is because that way of analysing the speech begins at the wrong place. It begins by assuming that Paul is trying to make a philosophical argument for one type of god. But, as we've seen, the Areopagus wasn't a debating society. It was a court. Paul's speech is an answer to the charge of bringing in foreign divinities.

If we begin from that point, we will see that some of his arguments are quite close to the arguments of a certain type of 'natural theology'. His underlying point is that he couldn't be bringing in foreign divinities *because the God he was proclaiming was already being worshipped at Athens*, albeit in ignorance. This true God had indeed been glimpsed by poets, even though the philosophers had got him wrong. The God he was proclaiming could not be foreign, since he already had a shrine in the city. Once people realised who he was, they would realise that he was the creator and judge of all – and thus not, in other words, a Middle Eastern deity that Paul was trying to import into Athens. He was the God who already claimed the whole world, and who (to say it again) was already worshipped in Athens, even though in ignorance.

Ignorance! Paul may be sailing close to the wind here. That, after all, had been Socrates' point: everyone else thought they knew the answers, but he knew that he didn't. Actually, the charge of ignorance means that the Apostle is putting the Athenians on the same footing as his Judean contemporaries: they have a zeal for God, he says, but it is not according to knowledge.[2] So while the Athenians may be very religious, they admit their own ignorance by the existence of this altar to the unknown God. And with that we arrive at the central substance of the speech.

All this places Paul in a subtly different position from those in our own age who have written about 'apologetics'. That word is frequently used to refer to the attempt to win over unbelievers by

2   Romans 10:2.

rational argument, presented in a supposedly 'neutral' space or on 'neutral' grounds. We make arguments, we present our evidence, and we hope to convince the sceptic that they ought at least to give the Christian faith a second look. But for Paul in Athens (this may be quite relevant now for many believers in today's world) it was a matter of explaining the faith to a *hostile* audience who were already suspicious that 'Christianity' was a dangerous force in the world. It was about explaining that the gospel message was not going to be a 'foreign body' in the culture, to be rejected out of hand, but rather that it offered the key, already present but unrecognised, to a badly needed wisdom and truth.

We should not be surprised at this slant on what Paul was doing. Many in our world today assume that Christians are committed to believing dangerous nonsense. Anyone known to embrace the faith can easily be portrayed, in the supposedly well-ordered world of Western secularism, as introducing alien assumptions and allegiances. We today who, perhaps to our surprise, have to defend our right to our beliefs and our moral stance may learn from Paul what a wise defence might look like – and how it might turn, after all, into a genuine gospel message.

The speech makes four basic points: the unknown God; the critique of idols; outflanking the philosophers; and putting the world right. I will lay these out one by one.

The unknown God

Paul begins, as we have seen, by referring to something he's seen in the city: an altar to an unknown God. Despite what has often been suggested, this was not an attempt on Paul's part to find a 'fixed point' in the local culture from which he could build a theological argument. The point about the unknown God was that it was precisely *not* a 'fixed point'. It was, as it were, a question mark: an open window, looking out from within the culture to something or someone else, without knowing what that might be. Yes, says Paul, an unknown God – but therefore (remember the charge against him) not a *foreign* divinity. Rather, one that you implicitly acknowledge that you need to know.

Pause for a moment and move from Paul's world to ours. Where, we might ask, are today's altars to an unknown God? Not, to be sure, in the militant and shallow would-be Christian rhetoric which ignores both secularism and postmodernity and bulldozes its way ahead, trying to create a neo-puritanism, politically as well as theologically. That simply puts people off. No: today's signs of the unknown God are, almost by definition, more subtle, more oblique. There are certain big themes, ideals if you like, which people in all cultures know are important for human flourishing but which we all find difficult or puzzling. I have written about them elsewhere: justice, love, freedom and beauty, spirituality, power, and yes, our old friend Truth itself.[3] We all know they matter but we all mess them up. Thoughtful people in every culture puzzle over them. But the Christian message has the capacity, as Paul showed in Athens, to tell a larger story which makes sense both of why these things matter, why and how they have got twisted, and how that can ultimately be put right.

You can see that in the way an older Christian art or music still has the power to draw people in and open up new possibilities. Think of Handel's *Messiah*, or Bach's *St Matthew Passion*, or the great Renaissance paintings – which still resonate even with people who are quick to distance themselves from any specifically religious commitment. We see it in the UK and Europe in the ancient cathedrals where tourists often find, to their surprise, that they are struck with a sense of divine presence, making them want to stop and say a prayer. Our world is highly confused, but there are still signposts in various places, and they matter. As Paul insists elsewhere, God the Creator has not left himself without witness, even if humans routinely take the signs of God's provision and make them into small gods in their own right. Which brings us to the second topic in Paul's speech: idolatry.

---

3 See *HE*, ch. 7; and *BS*.

The critique of idols

Pagan worship in Paul's day was ubiquitous in every city, town, street and home. It occupied roughly the same position as electricity does in our world. To suggest that you might live without reference to the gods was simply weird, not just because everybody did it and it was woven into the fabric of life, but because everybody assumed that keeping the gods happy was vital for personal and civic well-being. Even those who didn't really believe all the pagan mythology knew that you had to keep the system going. As we saw already in another context, if there was a plague, a fire or a famine, anyone who hadn't been doing their religious duty would be instantly under suspicion. Likewise, anyone who was introducing foreign gods . . . leading people away from the proper civic gods.

In a city such as Athens the gods – the standard mainstream ones such as Zeus and Poseidon, and the local ones such as Athene – had their own shrines. In Athene's case this was one of the architectural wonders of the world, the Parthenon, there on the Acropolis to this day (though short of some of its marbles). And Paul declares, categorically, that this whole system is a nonsense. So, far from Paul introducing foreign gods, the Athenians have been worshipping non-existent ones. Verse 24: the God who made the world, he says, the lord of heaven and earth, doesn't live in man-made shrines. Please note: this too doesn't fit the idea that the speech is simply finding 'points of contact' among Paul's hearers. Declaring that the stunning works of Athenian architecture were a category mistake was hardly the way to win friends.

But Paul rams the point home, echoing centuries of Judean polemic. The true God doesn't need people to feed him. *He* is the one who feeds *us* with life and breath and everything else. And since – as the poet Aratus had suggested three centuries earlier – humans are in some sense God's offspring, it makes no sense to represent the deity with man-made gold, silver or stone carvings (verse 29). These idols too, like the shrines in which they stand, are a nonsense. Again, this is hardly designed to make his audience comfortable. As we've seen, when Paul wrote to the Thessalonians, at exactly this moment in his travels, he insisted that when someone became a Christian they 'turned . . . from idols, to serve a living and true God'.[4] In case we might wonder, turning from idols was difficult, complicated and risky. You would appear antisocial and worse. The Judeans had permission to stay away from idol-worship. But for non-Judean Christians it was different. And dangerous.

The point about idols is that they are parodies of the truth. The sun is powerful and important. The sea is powerful and important. The erotic impulse in humans is powerful and important. The civic pride and status of somewhere such as Athens is powerful and important. But Zeus, Poseidon, Aphrodite and Athene do not actually exist. They are parodies of the wise provision of the Creator God. They are not the truth. They are at best pointers to the truth. To mistake them *for* that truth is to embrace a lie. To worship them is to distort your own humanness.

One of the great myths of modern secularism is that it's a kind of neutral space, in which we navigate our way by using our unaided reason. But there is no neutrality. As Bob Dylan said, 'you gotta serve somebody'. And once secularism pushes traditional Christianity upstairs out of sight, other gods quickly come in to take its place. Again, moving from Paul's world to our own, certain things stand out.

A survey taken early in 2023 showed that more Americans than ever now regard money as the primary force in life. The god Mammon is alive and well. Millions make daily pilgrimages to his shrine. He demands sacrifices. Some of those sacrifices are human. And if you suggest we should stop worshipping him, that there might be more important motives than sheer financial profit, people look at you strangely, just like they looked at Paul.

But it isn't only Mammon. Aphrodite, the goddess of erotic love, is alive and well. She has millions of devotees. The pornography industry is one of the biggest winners of the internet revolution. Erotic attraction supersedes everything else. Chastity, marital

---

4 1 Thessalonians 1:9.

fidelity, the lives and proper upbringing of children and many other things are regularly sacrificed on Aphrodite's altar, even though novelists and poets will remind you that it doesn't work. The idols do not give the truly human life they appear to promise. That's the thing about idols: they demand everything, but in the end they enslave, dehumanise and kill you. The ubiquitous idols of our modern supposedly secular society claim the status of truth but are lying.

And it isn't enough to try to fight Aphrodite on the surface level, as some Christians attempt to do, by labelling some things 'sinful' and warning that people who do them will go to hell. (I dare say that the battle over abortion is really a proxy war over two false gods: Aphrodite, who insists that unrestrained sex is a must, and Mars, who represents male power and violence. Some forces in our culture are afraid of the one; some are afraid of the other. That's a no-win situation.) Sin itself is a symptom, not the root cause. Sin is what happens when you worship an idol and let it dictate your behaviour. Idolatry is the real problem. Modern Christianity has moralised everything; but what matters is worship.

The third in the trio, after money and sex, is power, coming down in the end to brute force and violence. Mars, the god of war, is alive and well, making close alliance with money – think of the profitable arms industry – and often with sex, with rape a standard military practice. From the vile obscenity of international war to the horror of yet another school shooting, Mars offers the kind of truth which Pontius Pilate knew about: the hollow 'truth' that says he can kill whom he likes. But this, too, is a lie. It is not the way to be genuinely human. God the Creator will hold it to account.

Suggesting today that we should stop worshipping Mammon, Aphrodite and Mars may seem as crazy as Paul suggesting that the Greek gods were a category mistake. Of course, as I said, money, sex and power are important. We can't do without them. But they are not gods, and to pretend that they are is to collude with great and dangerous lies. The truth is that the Creator God has made a world in which what we know as 'forces', and what the ancients imagined were gods, have their vital roles to play in genuine human life. But to be genuinely human – to reflect the image of the true God – you need to abandon the idols and worship him alone. That is central to all Christian apologetics.

So Paul moves from his friendly reference to the altar to the unknown God to his rejection of the classical gods. But he isn't content with denunciation. He tells them about the true God: the one who made heaven and earth. In the context of his speech for the defence, he is saying that he can't possibly be introducing foreign gods, because the God of whom he is speaking – the God revealed in Jesus and displaying his power in the resurrection – is the God of all the earth who is already out and about all over the place, including in Athens. It's just that they don't know him, and thus keep lurching instead towards the normal idols.

This true God, he says, doesn't live in man-made shrines. Nor does he need gifts or food; he is the one who gives all gifts to humans – life and breath and everything. What's more – neatly looping around the accusation of 'foreign gods' – he made the whole human race from a single ancestor, allotting the nations their places and times. (We should note that if the Church had paid attention to verse 26 then the tragedy of Christians supporting racism would never have happened.) And then, before the final denunciation of idols in verse 29, Paul holds out the mysterious possibility that this Creator God actually wants humans to reach out for him and find him, since he is not in fact far away.

This is where Paul's third strategy emerges. Having begun with the unknown God, and having denounced the world of the idols, he outflanks the philosophers.

Outflanking the philosophers

The ancient philosophers offered what they saw as grown-up versions of the older paganism. Most of them rejected the tales of the gods, in Homer and elsewhere, as incredible and unworthy. Instead, the Stoics and the Epicureans, who as we saw were debating with Paul in the marketplace, offered two alternatives. Though Paul doesn't mention them explicitly in the speech, we can watch him outflanking them.

Paul actually addresses three positions, not just two. Stoicism replaced the multiplicity of gods with the one divine force, in everything, around everything, animating everything and everyone. Some Stoics addressed this omnipresent divinity in prayer. But the problem with pantheism is that it cannot critique evil. In ordinary paganism, if bad things happen it's because some god is cross. But if the one god of Stoic pantheism is in everything, then our perceptions of 'good' and 'bad' are just a trick of the light. You just have to accept the way things are: grit your teeth and learn to be calm – which is what today most people mean by being Stoic. Alternatively, you are free to leave: the noble suicide is a Stoic ideal.

But Paul says No to all this. Yes – the true God is all around us, very close to us – but he is different from us, approaching us in love and wanting an I–Thou relationship. And, crucially, the Creator God knows that his world is out of joint, and he has fixed a day on which he will sort it all out. Here is the ancient Judean vision of God coming to put everything right, of the day when the sea and the hills and the animals in the field will sing for joy because YHWH is coming to judge the world, to make all wrongs right. That is a radically different story from the one the Stoics told.

Meanwhile the Stoics' classic opponents were the Epicureans. For them, the gods did exist, but they were a long way away, in their own sphere, and had nothing to do with our world. They didn't intervene down here: our world developed under its own steam. (This was the original 'evolutionary' doctrine, clearly articulated by Epicurus and particularly by the Latin poet Lucretius in the first century BC, retrieved finally in the eighteenth century.) There was no point in praying to the gods, since they didn't hear and wouldn't respond. Human life is what it is and the best thing to do is to make yourself as comfortable as you can: rational pleasure is the ultimate principle, and tomorrow, when you die, you die, with nothing left. No afterlife. Ancient Epicureanism was popular because it denied all the old myths about angry gods waiting to torture you in an afterlife. It became popular again in the modern world for the same reason, rejecting the old thundering threats of the medievals and the Puritans. And Paul's response is to speak of the Creator God who lovingly made everything, including humans, in order to dwell with them, to establish a relationship with them. Verse 27: he is not far from each one of us. Paul is building up to a full Judean and biblical picture of the truth. His underlying argument is that the philosophers have glimpsed part of it, but not the whole thing.

The third philosophical position he outflanks is that of the so-called Academics, the continuing school of Plato. For them, the riddles presented by the world had no clear solution. Neither the Stoics nor the Epicureans had won the argument. The best thing to do, then, was to keep the older religious customs going, partly to sustain the social fabric, and partly because there might just be some truth in them somewhere. Paul, in a deft move, joins up his critique of that semi-scepticism with his comments about the unknown God. Yes, he says (verse 30), there has indeed been a time of 'ignorance'. The full evidence was not yet in. But now the one God – who, to repeat, was not a 'foreign god' but was out and about, including in Athens – commands all people everywhere to repent, to turn back from their idolatry, in the light of the newly unveiled promise that he is going to call the whole world to account, to set all ancient wrongs right at last. How do we know this? Because God has appointed a man to be the judge of the living and the dead, revealing this by raising him from the dead. For Paul, the resurrection demonstrated that Jesus was Israel's Messiah; and in Israel's Scriptures, such as Psalm 2 or Isaiah 11, the coming Messiah would call the whole world to account. Jesus is validated as that Messiah through being raised from the dead.

These three philosophical positions are recognisable in our culture too. But there's a major difference. In the first century, the default position, for most, was some form of Stoicism. In our world, the default position, for most, is some form of Epicureanism. Modern secularism is basically ancient Epicureanism with a few scientific footnotes and an injection of the myth of 'progress'. Classic Epicureanism never included 'progress', since all events consisted only of the random swerve and collision of atoms. The modern version has mixed in a bit of Judean and Christian eschatology into the system. But instead of a traditional divinity guiding the course of events, it has been assumed that the world, under its own steam, is simply getting better and better – despite all the evidence to the contrary in recent centuries.[5] Thus the theory of 'natural selection', including 'the survival of the fittest', is assumed to operate in the world of human society and politics as well as in the natural world, producing a 'biopolitical' world which develops – and, supposedly, improves – all by itself. Weirdly, this belief persists today in many quarters despite the outbreak of new and horrible wars, the pandemic, the refugee crisis and not least the mounting evidence of looming ecological catastrophe.

Thus, for many today, the gods are absent, leaving the world to run itself how it wants. This has been a convenient doctrine for the modern Western world. Many people, especially now in the USA, modify this in the Academic direction: we aren't really sure about all the dogmas, but we'll keep the religion going because it holds society together.

Within the secularist retrieval of Epicureanism, the newer versions of ancient paganism have flourished, as I said before, partly because once people have said they don't believe in God, they don't recognise the idols for what they are. But of course, there are the great swirling philosophical and ideological currents of our time, under the loose headings of 'modernity' and 'postmodernity'. At the risk of over-simplification, let me put it like this.

The modernist movement imagined that we had now discovered the key to all the mysteries of the world. But the masters of suspicion – Marx, Freud and Nietzsche, representing money, sex and power – examined the hidden agendas and declared that the modernist claim to 'truth' was all along a self-serving grab for power. But this postmodern position, deconstructing so much that modernism took for granted, has nothing to put in its place. You can't live on suspicion alone. Within modernism, the idea of human

---

5   On Epicureanism in the modern Western world, see *HE*, ch. 1.

rights for the whole world was rooted in the Jewish and Christian traditions, though many today pretend otherwise. But within post-modernism, the rhetoric of 'rights' has abandoned those roots and degenerated into the shrill, brittle certainties of different 'special interests' and newly constructed 'identities'. With that, Truth itself deconstructs into 'my truth' and 'your truth'; and woe betide any-one (a lawyer, say!) trying to work out what really happened. And public discourse deconstructs into a new kind of 'left' and a new kind of 'right', with many Christians feeling themselves bullied into agreeing with the 'right' because they are told that the new 'left' is anti-Christian. This is a recipe not only for confusion but for danger.[6]

What might it mean for a Pauline Christian to outflank today's complex and confusing philosophical climate, to mount a multi-layered apologetic into the multilayered confusion? That's a question for a whole new book, but let me very briefly say three things.

First, despite what many believe, the modernist emphasis on science is to be welcomed *but not in its Epicurean mode*. We need to separate carefully the delighted exploration and analysis of God's creation – which was always a Christian impulse – from the eighteenth-century embrace of a philosophy which assumed that God was out of the picture and that the world made itself in ran-dom fashion. Thus biological *evolution* as such is a genuine scien-tific finding; but evolution*ism*, the dogma that denies any divine involvement, is a philosophical a priori which science could never demonstrate. In my own field, the modernist emphasis on his-tory – on serious research into what actually happened, including the events that lie behind the Gospels – is not only to be welcomed; it is vital for healthy faith. But the assumption of many historians, from David Hume and Edward Gibbon in the eighteenth century to the so-called 'Jesus Seminar' in the twentieth, that 'historical' research will reveal a world without divine presence and activ-ity, with a merely human Jesus and a self-serving Church, is just that, a baseless assumption. So that's the first point: to give the

---

6   See my *JP* (with Michael F. Bird).

modernist Enlightenment its due, while challenging its philosophical assumptions.

Second, we have to welcome the postmodern critique but work through it and out the other side. I have long thought that the providential point of postmodernity was to preach the doctrine of the Fall to modernist arrogance, to show that all our epistemological righteousness was simply filthy rags. But this doesn't mean that there is no such thing as knowledge. The biblical vision of the human vocation includes – as with Adam naming the animals – the call to speak words that bring God's order into the world. And part of that wise ordering is recognising the *identity* of humans as made in God's image, male and female. Postmodernity is like a machine set up to deconstruct modernist arrogance, but without an 'off' button. When it carries on to deconstruct all human knowledge and identity, we must be able to offer an alternative. If we don't, we leave ourselves dangerously open to the clever lies of the demagogues, all the more attractive because of their slick presentation on social media.

The need to be able to offer an alternative applies especially, third, to the postmodern critique of all metanarratives. Yes, many big stories within modernity have been self-serving power-plays. But the Christian gospel, by definition, is not a power-play. It is a love story, the story of the Creator's love for his world, acted out in Jesus and now at work through the spirit. Tragically, Christians have often tried to turn the faith into a power-play, the triumph of one brand of faith over supposed enemies. But that is to collude with the world's power-narratives. Many – particularly the younger generation – see straight through it. That is one reason why many younger people want nothing to do with the faith. Our equivalent of Paul's critique of his philosophical climate must then be to demonstrate in action the truth of the love story which is God's ongoing relationship with his world.

So Paul's positive message is an Athens-friendly version of his normal theme: the *Judean* story, with Jesus as its climax. God the *Creator* longs and intends that, even in their ignorance, people might reach out and find him. This isn't a 'natural theology' in the sense of starting with the world and arguing logically up to the true God. It remains a Judean account of the non-Judean world, seen through the messianic lens. Pagan ignorance is confronted with Israel's Messiah. In Jesus, God has revealed his true self – and his true purpose, to put the world right, to 'judge' it in that sense. The Creator God will not for ever leave his creatures in ignorance. The altar to the unknown God constitutes a silent request. You can't argue from that up to the gospel, but when the gospel arrives it answers it in overflowing abundance. I earlier mentioned a bleak line of R. S. Thomas, and here's a much more positive one: he speaks of his whole being overflowing with God, as a chalice would with the sea.[7]

So, by the end, Paul has worked back to his usual message, as in 1 Thessalonians 1: you turned from idols to serve a living and true God, and to wait for his son Jesus, the deliverer. This is Jesus-focused *creational* monotheism; and – apologists again take note – it can take on board and recontextualise all that the pagan world could come up with. In 2 Corinthians 10:5, Paul describes this approach in terms of his intention to 'take every thought prisoner and make it obey the Messiah'.

So we can stand back and see what Paul has done. He was in the dock on a dangerous charge. But, in defending himself, he has reversed the roles. The Athenians thought they were judging him, but they were wrong. God is the judge (verse 31); and they, the Athenians, will be called to account by the resurrected Jesus. And that leads directly to the fourth and final point.

Putting the world right

It isn't enough to point to the altars to the unknown God, to denounce the idols and to engage with the philosophers. The Christian story of the world needs to be heard. This is the story of the world being put right at last. So many in our world assume that Christianity systematically distorts the world, and that we need to push it off the table so we can do a better job of sorting things out.

---

7   R. S. Thomas, 'Suddenly'.

If well-meaning Christians respond to this with the shrill assertion of a traditional faith, but without seeing how it actually works, that just makes things worse and more polarised.

Western Christianity of all varieties has normally assumed that the point of the story is for people to go to heaven when they die. But that is the view, not of Jesus or Paul, but of Plato and his followers. For Paul, as in this speech, the point of the biblical story is for God to come and dwell with us. And that requires – as the Bible insists, and as Paul declares starkly here – that God will in the end put all things right. The word 'judge' here often misleads, because we hear it negatively, as in God being angry. Well, God is indeed angry with all that defaces and distorts his beautiful world and his image-bearing creatures. But in the Bible 'to judge' means 'to put everything right', to sort it all out. That's why, in the Psalms (such as, for instance, numbers 96 and 98), all creation will celebrate because YHWH is coming to 'judge' the world – not to burn it up, but to put it all right. In whatever field we find ourselves working, our assumption must be, with Paul, the goodness of creation, the providence and personal presence of the Creator God, and the eventual goal of all things being put right. This is of course quite a stretch, but the anchor for it all is Jesus himself. Christian apologetics has often tried to prove the existence of God first and then to put Jesus into the frame, but the New Testament does it the other way round. Instead of trying to address a world of rationalism with rational arguments for God, we must address the world of deconstruction with the truth, and the love, of Jesus himself, and the new creation which has come into being with him.

This means, of course, Jesus' resurrection. We need to be clear. 'Resurrection' was never a fancy way of saying that Jesus 'died and went to heaven'; or that his kingdom-project continued despite his death; or that God loves us despite everything. 'Resurrection' in the ancient world always meant people who had been bodily dead being now bodily alive again. And here's the point: everybody in the ancient world knew that that didn't happen. It isn't that they didn't know the laws of nature and so were prepared to swallow all kinds of odd rumours. Christianity was born into a world where its central claim was bound to appear ridiculous. Just as Pontius Pilate sneered at Jesus' claim to be telling the truth, so the learned judges in Athens ridiculed Paul.

But there is something else going on here. Many have pointed out a particular irony at the end of Paul's speech. By insisting that everything turns on Jesus' resurrection, he is flying directly in the face of what the god Apollo had said in the legendary founding of the Court of the Areopagus itself, as described in the tragedy of Orestes, written by the first great fifth-century tragedian, Aeschylus.

In this play, *The Eumenides*, Orestes is on trial (as I mentioned earlier) for murdering his mother – even though he was doing so to avenge his father, in line with Apollo's specific instructions. As in many societies ancient and modern, there was then a real danger of a cult of vengeance going on and on, the *lex talionis* of an eye for an eye and so on, with every murder needing to be followed by another one.

So what's going to happen to Orestes? He is pursued by the Furies, who seem to be a kind of mythologised version of his own conscience. He flees to Delphi, where Apollo's oracle tells him to go to Athens. And there, making a long and complicated story short and simple, Apollo and Athene set up the Court of the Areopagus. This version of the legend, in one form or another, was well known in Paul's day. Indeed, Nero himself had played Orestes on stage, perhaps seeking to assuage public disapproval because he, too, had killed his own mother.

In the play, however, the Furies had declared that the blood-curse would have to go on, because once the mother's blood had drained out on the ground it couldn't be brought back (258–69). The only way to resolve things would then be through death itself, since Hades, the god of the dead, would square all accounts in the end (270–4). Orestes must therefore suffer the death penalty.

That is a bleak vision indeed, and Apollo isn't having it. He turns the argument against them. They want Orestes killed, but Apollo says that's too harsh, because, yes, once the dust has drunk a man's blood, that's it; *there is no resurrection* (655–6). He therefore pleads for mercy. The solemn Athenian judges then vote, and the vote is tied. But Athene has a casting vote, and votes to acquit Orestes. The play ends in a celebration: that here in Athens, here in the Court of the Areopagus, there is a wise and humane justice to be had, far superior to the endless *lex talionis* that would otherwise perpetuate a blood-feud on and on through the generations.

So when Paul speaks of Jesus' resurrection, as the guarantee that the God who raised him is indeed going to judge the world justly, Paul appears to be deliberately denying what Apollo had said about there being no resurrection. This has been pointed out often enough, and it seems to be right. But I think Paul is doing something far more interesting than simply telling Apollo, and Aeschylus, that they were wrong to deny resurrection. He is offering the Judean and biblical vision of God's ultimate justice, in order to outflank the Athenian claim that their high court was the last word in justice and mercy.

The whole speech is in fact deeply Judean. It stretches from creation to final judgement, focusing unsurprisingly on resurrection, which is where you're bound to land if you believe in the good creation and the ultimate just judgement. Paul is announcing the Creator God, speaking of him precisely not as a foreign god, but as the one whom they don't know but who is in fact present in their midst and sovereign over their futures. When Paul speaks in verse 31 of 'full and proper justice', he is claiming that what Athene had tried to do was a mere pale shadow of what the true God would do.

Thus, as Paul turned the tables on the Philippian magistrates, and as earlier Stephen had turned the tables on his judges in the Sanhedrin, so Paul now switches roles. He has been the defendant, but his defence is so successful, critiquing the culture and outflanking the philosophers on the way, that he is now holding the great Court of the Areopagus itself to account. There is a greater justice, enfolding a greater mercy. The law of the endless *lex talionis*, the blood-feud, is finished as the crucified Jesus is raised from the dead.

Inevitably, some of Paul's hearers sneer. Happily, some want to hear more. But the point is that he gets away free. '[He] went out from their presence' (verse 33). Luke doesn't say whether there was an official verdict; perhaps they just agreed to adjourn. But the force of Paul's overall argument remains: the true God, the Creator, the God we know in Jesus, is already at work, not at all a 'foreign god', not to be angrily dismissed as a blight on a secular culture or an unwelcome intruder representing an alien culture, but rather 'not far from each one of us' (verse 27). Having made all humans from one stock, he now calls all to turn from their idolatry and discover him as their wise and redeeming father. Paul has moved from defence to critique to apologia to evangelism to a grand outflanking of the very basis of the highest court in the most civilised city in his world. This speech draws together the large strategy of his Gentile mission, assuming the Judean view that all the world belongs to the one Creator, that all people are on a level before him, and that he will one day put all things right. And the Creator God will do that not, like Hades, by bringing all down to the gloom of death; not, like Athene, by a clever mixture of justice and mercy; but, through Jesus, by the new creation which was launched in his resurrection and in which all shall be put right at the last.

Conclusion

The main theme in Acts 17 – 20, then, has been Paul's ministry to the pagan world. In Paul's speech in Athens, we detect the haunting possibility that the pagan ignorance of the true God might yet provide, paradoxically, the starting point for the gospel message. Paul has drawn out the significance of the altar to an 'unknown God'; he has critiqued the culture of idolatry, engaged with the philosophers, and told once more the true story of the world, focused on Jesus and his resurrection. Facing the supreme court in Athens, he has unveiled the true justice that will put the world right in the end.

Our difficulties and confusions today might be summarised like this. Some Christians have been so afraid of idolatry that they never notice the altars to the unknown God, leading them to warn against any attempt to see the true God in the sunrise or the smile of a child. Others have been so eager to embrace and affirm anything that looks vaguely 'religious' that they ignore or forget the real problem of idolatry, of religion 'gone bad'. That either/or – lurching from nervous fear to over-eager embrace and back again – represents a major fault line. For the over-cautious conservative today, Jesus' resurrection functions simply as a grand miracle that proves the existence of a 'supernatural' interventionist deity, rather than the inauguration of the new creation for which the old world has been longing. For the over-eager liberal, the idea of Jesus' resurrection can only be a metaphor for a vague affirmation of God's benevolence, or his kingdom-project. These misunderstandings play out in Western culture in terms of political battles, with ignorant armies clashing by night.

Something similar happens in relation to Paul's third and fourth themes. Some today are so keen to engage with contemporary philosophy and culture that they forget how the biblical story actually works, and they produce a philosophically framed version of the faith with occasional biblical decoration. Others are so eager to proclaim the biblical story as they see it that they ignore the challenge to engage with contemporary culture and ideas. That stand-off, too, represents a fault line today between philosophical (or systematic) theology and biblical studies, as well as between wider forces in our culture. We urgently need to address this within an overarching commitment to the truth of God and his creation and in the context of a genuine, enquiring, robust faith.

So what then is the faith for which Paul is arguing? Many in today's sceptical world have the impression that 'faith' means turning the clock back to an easier time where the answers were given in advance and you didn't have to think. 'Faith' like that then becomes a protective shield against the truth that other people are investigating and articulating. I am suggesting – as Paul was suggesting to *his* sceptical audience – that genuine Christian faith, anchored in the revelation of new creation in Jesus' resurrection, means faith in the Creator God, made known in Jesus, now embracing the whole world of creation and providence, of the strange and loving nearness of God to his human creatures, and of his promise to put all things right at the last.

Pontius Pilate had sneered at Jesus' claim. The Athenian judges ridiculed Paul. Many of our contemporaries today dismiss the Christian message, not least because of the shrill and shallow distortions on display in many places. But the dangerous truth of God's new creation is at work still. Our task in this next generation is to grasp, in faith, the larger world that the gospel reveals. We are called to explore it with delight; to expound and explain it at every opportunity; and especially to express it through the works of mercy, beauty, wisdom and justice which, in displaying the new creation in advance, bear the unmistakable fingerprints of the risen Jesus.

In William Golding's last novel *The Double Tongue*, the heroine is the priestess of Apollo at Delphi. She has been Apollo's slave, inhaling hallucinatory vapours and then answering, in hexameters, the personal or political questions that people ask, including one from the young Julius Caesar. When she was younger, she had found Apollo to be a violent, frightening reality. But for years now, she has felt the old gods withdrawing, leaving behind them a void – but that void itself has seemed somehow full of gentle mystery. In her old age, the rulers of Athens, grateful for her long service at Delphi, write to say that they want to put up a statue of her. She thinks back to the void after the wild gods had gone: a sense of something different, inexplicably tender and benign. No, she says, don't put up a statue to me. Please just build a simple altar, and inscribe it with the words: 'to the unknown God'.

8
Acts 21 – 24

Trouble in Jerusalem

Introduction

I've heard it said that a good novel, or indeed a great play, should be read three times: first to discover 'what happens', second to ponder the characters and their motives; then, third, to ask bigger questions about what it all means.

That's especially true in a passage such as Acts 21 – 24. It's so full of exciting detail that it's easy just to sit back and watch the film (so to speak) without really getting the point. So let's do a first quick skim: Acts 21 – 24 from 40,000 feet.

We start with getting Paul back to Jerusalem after his wanderings, only to be faced with yet another riot. That's chapter 21. Paul then tries to explain himself to the crowd, only to make matters worse to the point where the soldiers have to rescue him; that's chapter 22. Chapter 23 starts with a hearing before the Sanhedrin, continues with a plot against Paul's life, and ends with the Romans taking Paul away to the comparative safety of Caesarea, down by the coast. That's where the Roman governor, Felix, lives and holds court, and chapter 24 sees Paul appearing before him, without any great decisions being made. That sets us up for chapter 25, in which Paul gets tired of waiting and, faced with Felix's successor, Festus, appeals to Caesar. This then takes the plot forward to its goal.

In a sense, then, these four chapters don't take us very far. Paul gets to Jerusalem and then to Caesarea; that's it! But they tell us a great deal about the inner meaning of it all, which prepares us to understand the closing scenes, and thereby to see more deeply into the book as a whole.

Paul goes to Jerusalem

So let's take that survey down from 40,000 feet to about 10,000, and see what we now notice. In chapter 21, Paul leaves Miletus, having addressed the Ephesian elders and given them some quite stark warnings. Verses 1–14 of the chapter detail the stopping-places on the voyage, making quite a contrast with the end of chapter 18 where Luke summarises a similar journey in much quicker time. The fact that he's slowed this one down tells us that he wants to highlight something, and it's not hard to see what it is: it's the repeated warnings to Paul that bad things are going to happen to him in Jerusalem. The disciples at Tyre tell him not to go (verse 4). The prophet Agabus warns (verse 11) that he will be tied up and handed over to the Gentiles – echoing the predictions of Jesus about what was going to happen to him. (I think that's quite deliberate on Luke's part: he is building up to a climax, but also teasing any first-time readers into guessing wrongly, into thinking that perhaps Paul is indeed going to be killed as Jesus was.) So (verses 12–14), all the people with Paul urge him not to go to Jerusalem. He appears to confirm our wrong guesses by saying that yes, he's ready to go to the city and, if need be, to die there.

When they arrive, there is something of a lull. Paul visits James, as he was bound to do. He tells him and all the elders about the extraordinary things God has been doing in the Gentile world. I suspect Paul was as frustrated by James's response as I am when I read what he says in verses 20–5. Paul has just explained the multiple ways in which the gospel has been at work in the Gentile world. But all James and his close associates can think about is the likely effect when zealous folk in Jerusalem discover that the man at the centre of the dangerous rumours has come to town. It reminds me of that moment in the film *Amadeus* when Emperor Joseph hears Mozart's stunning new opera and says that, though he has quite enjoyed it, there are 'too many notes'. If only Mozart would cut a few of them out, it would be perfect. In the same way, if only Paul could quieten down all this stuff about God including Gentiles . . . which of course was, for Paul, the quintessence of the gospel of grace.

Now of course I sympathise with James too. We will return to that presently. James knows only too well what the tensions in Jerusalem are like, and the way in which any mention of Paul will be like a match thrown into a box of fireworks. But Paul goes along with his suggestion of undergoing a rite of purification. As in 1 Corinthians 9:20, 'I became like a Judean to the Judeans': James is concerned that Paul should be perceived as a good torah-abiding Judean, and Paul goes along with it (despite the other bits of 1 Corinthians 9, about being 'like someone lawless to the lawless'). I suspect that Paul would be saying under his breath 'I do it all because of the gospel' and 'I have become all things to all people, so that in all ways I might save some' – while also wishing that James would see the same point.

Anyway, he undergoes a rite of purification, along with some other pilgrims doing the same thing. Seven days pass – nervous ones, no doubt, for everyone concerned. But then the balloon goes up (verses 27–35).

The tactic devised by James fails because some Judeans from Asia (in other words, from western Turkey, the district focused on Ephesus) see Paul in the Temple. They had already seen Trophimus, a Gentile from Ephesus, in Jerusalem with Paul, and they guessed, wrongly, that Paul had taken him into the Temple, in defiance of the 'no Gentiles' rule. They incite a riot, shouting – and this, of course, is very significant – that Paul teaches everybody everywhere 'against our people, our law, and this place' – that is, the Temple. Luke's reader will pick up echoes of the anger against Stephen back in chapter 7; but the same reader will realise that, no matter how carefully Paul in his own teaching and writing expressed himself, that is how his mission would be perceived.

I am always surprised, when I read this passage, that Paul escaped with his life. The mob grabbed him and were beating him, until (verses 31–6) the Roman soldiers came to rescue him. The predictions of his friends as he was travelling to Jerusalem might easily have come true.

Anyway, the tribune in charge of the soldiers assumes that Paul is a lower-class troublemaker, one of whom he has already had wind; so he's surprised when Paul speaks Greek to him. And Paul – being Paul – isn't done yet. He had hoped, as we saw, to be in Jerusalem for a big festival, presumably so that he could address the crowds. Well, now's his chance, bruised and bleeding though he may be after the attack by the mob. So, in verses 37–40, he persuades the tribune to let him speak.

(This leads to a splendid moment at the end of the chapter. Whoever did the chapter divisions broke off chapter 21 right where Luke has set Paul up to speak. In the older days in the Church of England the readings in the official lectionary used to work through chapter by chapter, week by week, in the Authorized King James Version, stopping where the chapter stopped. So, if you had been in church at this point, you would have heard: 'And when there was made a great silence, he spake unto them in the Hebrew tongue, saying, *Here Endeth the Second Lesson.*')

Anyway, in Acts 22:1–21, we have Paul's attempt at a defence. He tells the story of the Damascus Road, taking care to include various elements to show that he and the others involved were good loyal Judeans. But, at the point where Jesus tells Paul that he's sending him to the Gentiles, the crowd riots again. The very thought of the pagan world is, it seems, enough to set them off, even if it's Israel's Messiah himself who is giving these unexpected instructions. (Of course, that by itself would be enough to make them doubt whether such a Jesus could actually be Israel's Messiah.) So the tribune wants to do the usual Roman thing, which was to torture the prisoner in order to get to the truth (verses 22–30). But that too is quickly broken off when, as in Philippi, Paul reveals his Roman citizenship. So the tribune, still puzzled as to what it's all about (by this point Luke's readers may be wondering the same thing!), brings him to the Sanhedrin. That takes us to the start of chapter 23.

Faced with the Sanhedrin, Paul effectively does what he did in Athens, turning the tables on his accusers. Then, after a word of encouragement from Jesus himself (verse 11), some zealots make a plot against his life, which his nephew discovers (verses 12–22). This is another of those moments when we want to stop Luke and say, 'Hold on, how many relatives does Paul have living there? Are they believers?' And so on. We just don't know. Anyway, rather than risk Paul's life (verses 23–33), the tribune sends his awkward prisoner by night to Caesarea, to the Roman governor Felix.

Then finally, in chapter 24, there's an abortive legal hearing before Felix. It's abortive for two reasons: the actual charge isn't clear, and the main witnesses aren't there. That, one might suppose, does rather get in the way of a trial process. But this then leads to a lull. Felix keeps Paul in custody for two years, hoping that he might be able to get a bribe out of him. (Paul had, after all, brought a large sum of money with him to Jerusalem, and it's quite likely that word of this had leaked out.) Felix, whose wife is Judean, has regular conversations with Paul, rather (we may suppose) like Herod Antipas having frequent conversations with John the Baptist.[1] But Paul's teaching about 'justice, self-control and the judgment to come' (verse 25) scares Felix, and nothing comes of it. Then, finally, Felix's term of office comes to an end, and he is replaced by Porcius Festus.

So much going on; so many moving parts.

Who is involved?

Next, we ask who's involved, and what's in it for them.

Start with Rome. Rome was active in the Middle East partly because it was a buffer zone against the great eastern enemy, Parthia. In addition, Rome was overcrowded, and the local Italian farms couldn't keep up with the necessary food production; so they needed to get their regular supply of grain from Egypt. The trade routes in the eastern Mediterranean therefore had to be kept clear.

---

1 Mark 6:20.

So Rome's main aim was to keep the lid on any Middle Eastern trouble.

Rome normally ran things through local elites, letting them do the dirty work. That's why Herod the Great had been made king of the Jews: he was the biggest thug around. Rome would, however, normally have a prefect – a senior Roman official – in overall charge. The prefect (as we just saw with Felix) was based in Caesarea, down on the coast, though coming up to Jerusalem for major events. Unsurprisingly, there was regularly tension between Rome and those local elites, in this case the chief priests and the successive Herods. The prefects themselves were regularly corrupt, feathering their nests in the hope of a comfortable retirement. But they in turn were also afraid of the locals sending a bad report to the emperor and getting them into trouble. It's worth remembering, too, that the prefects had a good spy network. They knew what was going on among revolutionary groups. And that brings us to the Judean people.

The Judeans were fed up with being ruled by pagans, as they had been for most of the previous half-millennium. Many were eager for God to become King on earth as in heaven. They cherished the biblical prophecies of restoration and renewal, hoping that, if they remained loyal to torah and Temple, God would act at last. Torah and Temple – the symbols of God's presence with his people, and of his promises to redeem them at last – were like the national flags. Any threat towards them would spark instant anger and reaction. Revolutionary and/or messianic movements came and went, with some hard-line Pharisees in support. As we saw earlier, Gamaliel refers to some such movements in chapter 5.

This combination of Rome's aims and Jewish ferment is already toxic, without any help from Paul. But there are two more elements.

First, Jerusalem would fill to bursting point several times a year for the great festivals. Passover celebrated Israel's liberation from slavery in Egypt; Pentecost evoked the giving of torah and tabernacle. But the Diaspora Jews, pouring into the city like summer tourists in Oxford, had their own agendas. Just as some British expats in other countries become 'more British than the British', insisting on tea at 4 o'clock and carefully following the cricket scores, so many Judeans in the Diaspora became 'more Judean than the Judeans', holding in their minds an idealised picture of Jerusalem, the Temple and the pure community keeping the holy torah. Back home in the Gentile world, they had the precarious status (which varied from place to place, but was more or less accepted) of being a 'permitted religion', at least to the extent of their being allowed not to participate in the worship of other deities. They were all the more keen to practise their own religion, to show their real identity and to avoid compromise. But, as we saw, Paul's missionary work was challenging that legal status of 'permitted non-participation', claiming it equally for the multi-ethnic followers of Jesus. The finer points of all this would pass most Diaspora Judeans by. All that most of them knew about Paul was the rumour that he was 'against torah and Temple'.

As for the Jerusalem Christians, who after chapter 21 keep in the background, they were easily caught in the crossfire. They were poor, having pooled their resources. They were politically suspect, because, following Jesus' teaching, they refused to join violent resistance movements. That was bad enough. But ever since Stephen, the Jerusalem Christians had themselves been labelled as anti-Temple, perhaps also anti-torah – despite their visible piety. And now the word on the street was that their friend Paul had been going around the Diaspora telling Jews they didn't have to keep torah. So the accusation of disloyalty, undermining the hope of Israel, hung over the Jerusalem Christians too like a bad smell.

And now their supposed friend Paul had come back. They were naturally anxious. That's why they dreamed up the careful plan in Acts 21:17–26, which, as we saw, didn't work. Indeed, it backfired, by putting Paul in the Temple where he was open to misunderstanding and accusation.

But Paul, too, had a story in his heart and his head.

It's easy to forget, when we read Acts 20 – with Paul on the move, going from Ephesus to Corinth, then back round through Macedonia, and finally off to Jerusalem – that one of the last things he did in Corinth, just a few weeks earlier, was to write a theological symphony in four movements. We call it Romans.

Romans celebrates the saving love of God in the gospel of his son. It also laments the failure of most of Paul's fellow Judeans to believe in that gospel. In chapters 9 – 11, Paul works through the tears, the prayers and the hopes which he constantly experiences on this score, and he speaks in the end of parading, celebrating, his Gentile ministry before his fellow Judeans, in the hopes of making some of them jealous – jealous that the Gentile nations were inheriting *their promises*! – and so drawing them to faith (11:13–14). His argument in chapter 11 is carefully built up on the foundations earlier in the letter: they are the Messiah's people according to the flesh, and the messianic pattern is to be repeated in their coming to faith.[2]

This of course has been misunderstood in our own times. Some have supposed that Paul was imagining a large-scale last-minute conversion of all or most Judeans, perhaps then heralding the return of Jesus and/or the end of the world. That's implausible. He was, after all, intending to go on to Rome and then to Spain. No: the hope he expresses in Romans 11 is that he will save *some*. That was the narrative in Paul's head as he arrived back in Jerusalem.

So he had come with a substantial gift of money – collected for the church, he says in his letters, but in Acts 24:17 he tells Felix that it was intended more generally for 'my nation'. He had been hurrying precisely to be there for the crowds at Pentecost. What was he thinking? He was hoping that by bringing money from Gentiles, who, as Scripture had said they would, had abandoned idolatry and were now monotheists worshipping Abraham's God in the name of Israel's Messiah, he might be able to persuade some local Jerusalem Judeans, *and* perhaps some Diaspora pilgrims, to accept the gospel.

So one of the most frustrating moments in these chapters comes at chapter 22:21. Paul, telling the crowds his own story, has built it up very carefully, emphasising his continuing loyalty to Israel's God. He has highlighted his background as a loyal Judean, and his earlier efforts to stamp out the new heretical movement. He has stressed the holiness of Ananias and the God-given message he passed on (verses 14–16, looking back to 9:10–19). He has developed

---

2   See esp. *PFG*, ch. 11; summarised in *PB*, pp. 331–5.

his story to the point where, following the train of thought in Romans, he must have been ready to explain how the Scriptures themselves, torah itself, are now fulfilled in God's messianic gospel for the wider world, including, as a reflex action, God's fresh purposes for ethnic Judeans too. He must have been eager to explain, as in Romans 15, how the money he'd collected was a sign and token of that larger promise, and of a new kind of extended eschatological Israel, led by Israel's Messiah, who had embodied Israel's hope in being raised from the dead . . .

But he can't get beyond the word 'Gentiles'. He stands there after verse 21, with Romans 9 – 11 and 12 – 16 in his heart and almost on his lips, protected ironically by Roman soldiers, while the crowds are shouting, tearing their clothes, and tossing dust in the air, symbolically rejecting his supposed blasphemy. And then he's back in the barracks, about to be tortured. And that's the last time Paul gets to speak to the crowd. Their angry rejection is exactly the sort of thing he'd been talking about – and weeping over – in Romans 9.

No doubt James and the others, listening to the riot from a safe distance, are shaking their heads and wishing, as they did back in chapter 9, that he'd never come. And we never get to hear what actually happened to the famous collection. Did James and the others reject it because it was 'tainted money'? Did Paul find an appropriate way to hand it over? We don't know. Did it change the minds of any Jerusalem Christians? I'm sorry to say that I rather doubt it.

The meaning behind the narrative

So what is Luke telling us in all this? He has written these chapters as a fast-paced, rollicking good story. But at the end of chapter 24, it runs out of steam. That, like 22:21 with Paul's mention of Gentiles and the renewed riot, is a major anti-climax. If it feels like that for us, think how it was for Paul. He had come with the collection. He was eager then to go on to Rome and then Spain . . . and now he cools his heels for *two years* in a Roman prison, probably quite a nice one as prisons go but still not what he wanted, or expected or prayed for. If you want to make God laugh, people say, tell him your plans. (Mind you, the corollary to that is, if you want to make God weep, tell him you haven't got any.)

So what is Luke doing? And how do we move from the narrative, through the characters, to the meaning?

As always, Luke writes as an artist. He has given us an attractive picture of Paul: Paul the beloved pastor, praying with his friends, groups of whom are keen for him to stay, to protect him from danger. Luke has allowed us to see into Paul's heart as he reflects on his travels and missionary work. In doing this, Luke echoes biblical themes, and also, tellingly, themes from the life of Jesus. The prophecies about the danger facing Paul in Jerusalem remind us of Jesus' own warnings about his forthcoming death. A first-time reader, as we saw, might imagine that Paul was indeed going to be killed as Jesus had been. But in this case 'being handed over to the Gentiles' turns out to mean, not crucifixion, but rescue from the mob! So there is irony as well as parallel. After all, this story is not about *Paul* dying a once-for-all death for the sins of the world. It is about the way that the victorious death of Jesus is then *implemented* in the progress of the gospel, including apostolic suffering. We'll see more about that in our final chapter.

But there are also parallels with the story of Stephen's trial and martyrdom, which focused particularly on the Temple. Here Paul, following ironically in Stephen's footsteps, claims the theological high ground. He is loyal to the biblical tradition. Stephen had spelled it out in considerable detail, retelling the large biblical story; Paul, as we know, was well capable of doing the same thing. He claims to be faithful to that tradition. But it's the present Jerusalemites who are in rebellion against their God and the messianic fulfilment of his age-old promises.

Through all this, then, Luke is insisting that Paul, despite popular impressions, has all his life been loyal to Israel's God, to the Law and the Prophets, *and he still is*. That is one of the main underlying messages of both Acts and Romans. Granted, as in Galatians, torah itself was to be seen as a temporary dispensation; its requirement for Gentiles to be circumcised is now done away with for those who have believed and been baptised. But the Law and the Prophets do indeed bear witness to the gospel. As a result – and this is Paul's big point – *following Jesus the Messiah is the way to be a genuinely loyal Judean.* You see that in the third chapter of his letter to the Philippians, where, though at one level Paul declares that he's abandoning his Judean privileges, he goes on at once to celebrate the hope of the resurrection because of the work of the Messiah – in other words, to refer to the fulfilment of the single great Judean story, and to claim that it is fulfilled in Jesus.

The crucial point, of course, is Jesus' resurrection. Here, as in Romans, it's the resurrection that validates Jesus' messiahship. Everything else follows from that. By chapter 23, it seems that Paul had given up hope of expounding Romans 9 – 11 to suspicious Jerusalemites. That is clear from the plot against his life in chapter 23: the plotters had got authority from the chief priests for their plan to kill Paul, just as Saul of Tarsus himself had got authority from the chief priests to persecute the church, back in chapter 9! But it's the resurrection that changes everything. When he is addressing the high priest and the Council, he reduces everything to this one point. So, as with Acts 2, in Jesus' resurrection God has launched his new day, which now fulfils Israel's hopes. That is the point Paul was still eager to make. If he couldn't say it to the mob, he could at least say it to the Sanhedrin – and then, in the end, to King Herod Agrippa, as we shall see.

Throughout all this, Luke draws attention to the question: what exactly is the charge against Paul, and who is bringing it? Luke is probably preparing for Paul's forthcoming trial in Rome itself, or – if he's writing later – thinking of the charges that Christians continued to face.

To get clearer on all this, we retrace our steps. In chapter 21, the trouble kicks off at verse 27 when some Diaspora Judeans see Paul with a Gentile friend. They put two and two together and make seventeen, accusing him of having smuggled his friend into the Temple to pollute it – despite the fact that Paul had undergone a careful and somewhat 'staged' purification process in order to avoid just such a charge. The implicit accusation is clear. He is indeed fraternising with the polluted idolatrous pagans, with 'Gentile sinners'. That's what people had been saying about him for several years, because they couldn't grasp what he says in Galatians, that when a pagan comes to faith and gets baptised *that person is a 'Gentile sinner' no longer.* The Messiah's death has dealt with sin. All believers are on level ground – a point which the suspicious Jerusalemites, with the book of Daniel and the Maccabean history in folk memory, and the Romans bossing and bullying them in their own land, were never going to get, despite the earlier agreement in chapter 15.

So when Paul is then sent to the governor Felix, the tribune Lysias says (23:29) that the trouble concerned 'disputes about their law' – rather like what Gallio had said in Corinth in 18:14–15. (Luke's summary of the tribune's message in 23:27, with Lysias carefully omitting any mention of his original intention to torture Paul, shows him to be more than a little economical with the truth.) And when Paul then appears before Felix in chapter 24, the barrister Tertullus, hired by the chief priests, accuses him of being a rabble-rouser, a ringleader of the Nazarenes, and of trying to pollute the Temple (24:2–9). Those, vague as they are, seem to be the charges against him.

But in his defence in chapter 24, Paul pushes back at this very point. The accusation came from the Diaspora Judeans; why are they not here to testify? The accusers are unable either to settle on the charge or to present their witnesses. Anyone familiar with Roman law would see that Paul was running rings round them.

So Luke, throughout this complicated and fast-paced story, is hammering home the point: *Paul is a loyal Judean who shouldn't even be on a charge in the first place.* Yes: we recognise this theme; it goes all the way back to the Philippi magistrates, to the effective acquittal in Athens, to Gallio in Corinth, and to the town clerk in Ephesus. It is, of course, ironic. In Philippi and Ephesus, Paul was in trouble with pagans because he was a kind of Judean. In Corinth – as here – he's in trouble because the Judeans think he's the *wrong kind* of Judean, flirting with paganism. And it all stems from Paul's central belief, that Jesus, in his death and resurrection, has been marked out publicly as Israel's Messiah, so that God's new world has been inaugurated, with him as its rightful lord over the whole world. This new wine simply won't go into the old bottles.

That emerges strikingly in Paul's statement before Felix in 24:10–21. Everything Paul has been doing, up to and including this last trip to Jerusalem, has been out of loyalty to Israel's God, and out of the consequent hope for resurrection. (As we've seen before, resurrection is where you get to theologically if you believe in God as the good Creator and in God's purpose to put all things right at the end.) All this means that following Jesus wasn't so much a new *religion* as the unveiling of a new *reality*. But you wouldn't expect a Roman magistrate to see that point, any more than a Greek philosopher. Or, sadly, a zealous Jerusalem mob.

You can see the misunderstanding close up in 23:6–10. (We'll come back presently to the introduction to the scene in verses 1–5.) If you're going to believe in resurrection, you have to have some view on who or what humans still are *between bodily death and bodily resurrection.*[3] The Pharisees in this period had at least two theories: people in that intermediate state are perhaps like angels, or perhaps like spirits. Luke explains in verse 8 that the Sadducees did not believe in the resurrection, 'neither angel nor spirit' (literal translation), but, he says, the Pharisees acknowledge them *both*. The Greek here is *amphotera*, which does not mean 'all three' as NRSV and some other translations wrongly put it. It means 'both'. In other words, the Sadducees, who deny the resurrection, also deny either kind of intermediate state, whereas the Pharisees, who do believe in the resurrection, hold on to those two theories about existence in an 'angelic' and/or 'spirit' state between death and resurrection.

So the Pharisees then propose a more generous interpretation of Paul's point. They can't imagine that Paul really means what he says, namely that Jesus had *already* been bodily raised from the dead ahead of everyone else, launching God's new creation upon

---

3 On this passage, see esp. *RSG*, pp. 132–4.

the surprised and unready old world. So they say (in verse 9), that perhaps Paul had seen a vision of someone in the intermediate state, an 'angel' or a 'spirit'. We think back to the confusion in Athens when people thought Paul was talking about two new divinities, 'Jesus' and 'Anastasis'. Neither Judeans nor Greeks were ready for the great eschatological claim, so clear throughout Acts: that, with Jesus' actual bodily resurrection, a new creation has opened up which *fulfils* the true hope of Israel and therefore *challenges* the pagan world to repent and believe. We see that challenge put rather sharply in Paul's regular conversations with Felix and Drusilla in 24:24–7, which Felix breaks off when Paul challenges him about justice, self-control and the coming judgement.

Luke's reader knows all this. But neither party in the Sanhedrin will understand it, still less the Roman tribune or his boss, the governor. All they can hear is social unrest and political danger; just as the mob in the street can only hear an attack on Israel's cherished institutions, undermining their hope of God's kingdom – when the message was in fact about that kingdom already being inaugurated. New creation has been launched, and all they can do is to grumble because it doesn't look like their previous mental images of it. This is where C. S. Lewis's illustration might come in: they are like children who refuse a holiday by the seaside because they are playing with mud pies in a dirty yard and can't imagine anything better.

Conclusion

Where might all this leave us, reading Acts 21 – 24 today? We will celebrate the quick flashes of special divine providence. In 23:11, Jesus encourages Paul, telling him that he will indeed get to Rome; Paul surely needed that through those frustrating two years of waiting. In 23:16, Paul's nephew somehow caught wind of the plot: another nice providence. And so on. And we will be reminded, as throughout the book, that Jesus' resurrection is not simply one remarkable event among others, but is the lynchpin of the whole thing. Without the resurrection, Jesus is just another failed Judean leader; the world has not turned its vital corner; heaven and earth have not come together; YHWH has not returned to Zion, and the Romans and unbelieving Judeans are right to label Paul a crazy troublemaker.

In particular, Luke's presentation challenges the view of Paul which has become surprisingly popular recently, under the heading 'Paul within Judaism'. Its central proposal, that Paul thought believing in Jesus was a good thing for Gentiles but that Judeans could just stay torah-observant as they were, ignores the centre of Paul's thought – the crucified and risen Messiah – just as effectively as his hearers did in these chapters. As with the mob, the Sanhedrin and the Roman governor, it's a way of not paying attention to what the apostle is saying. Luke's portrayal of Paul as a paradoxically loyal though misunderstood Judean provides part of the best answer. What are you supposed to do, if you can see that the sun has risen but you're talking to people whose curtains are tight shut because they're afraid of the dark?

One tail-piece, tying in with an earlier theme. Chapter 23 offers another great example of Paul dealing with human authorities. Remember the line about 'obeying God rather than humans'? Remember how Paul reminded the Philippian magistrates how to do their own job? How he turned the tables on the Athenian judges? Well, here is Paul in front of the high priest. After his first sentence, the high priest orders a flunky to hit him in the mouth – a brutal way of saying, 'You shouldn't be speaking in your own defence'. Paul rebukes him: 'You striking *me*? Have a taste of the *lex talionis*: God will strike *you*!' The bystanders are horrified: you can't speak like that to the high priest! Paul hadn't realised who he was: this was a council meeting, and the high priest wouldn't be wearing official robes. In any case, after his long absence, Paul wouldn't know which member of the ruling clan happened to be holding office at that moment. But he accepts the point, and again responds with Scripture: it was a sin of ignorance. Had he known that this man was high priest, then a text from torah, Exodus 22:28, would have come into play: you must not speak evil of a ruler.

That, after all, is part of the political outflowing of creational monotheism. God wants his world to be stable and ordered under wise human governance. Even when the rulers are neither wise nor stable, one must treat them with respect. Paul, in other words, will respect the office, *but he reserves the right to tell the present holder of the office that he's out of line* – just as in Philippi. This is not, perhaps, the best way to gain people's affection. But that seems not to have been high on Paul's list of priorities.

All Paul's skills and strategies for potentially awkward situations will then be displayed in the final chapters. As we'll see presently, Luke brings the work to its conclusion with clear large-scale implications, as important today as they were then, about how God's gospel strategy will play out in the world.

9

Acts 25 – 28

And So to Rome

Introduction

What happens when we view Acts as a whole? In chapter 1, Jesus' ascension joins heaven and earth together, constituting him as lord of the world, and his followers are commissioned to be his witnesses to the ends of the earth. In chapter 28, Paul arrives in the capital of the present lord of the world, announcing God as king and Jesus as lord, boldly and with no one stopping him, to the great city and hence to the whole world.

In chapter 2, the rushing mighty wind fills the house, giving the disciples new words to speak of Jesus. Now, in chapter 27, we have another rushing mighty wind – but this time it's the fierce north wind sweeping Paul and his companions into mortal danger. Luke the artist knows his business. Those indwelt by God's spirit, proclaiming his mighty works to the world, will face the angry storms one way or another. Yes, says Luke, but God will bring you through. Acts, you see, is not after all the story of Paul. It's the story of *what Jesus has continued to do and to teach*: the story, in other words, of the gospel. So, though at the end of the book we want to know what happened to Paul, Luke doesn't mind disappointing us. He tells us what happened to the gospel. That's what matters. Remember that, any readers who are called to a life of ministry: what matters is not what happens to you, but what happens to the gospel, and *through* the gospel.

We then notice the parallel and contrast between chapter 4 and chapters 25 – 26. In 4:23–31 the apostles in prayer quoted Psalm 2, applying it to the fact that Herod and Pilate had conspired together with the people to put Jesus on the cross. Now in 25 – 26, the present (and last) Herod comes together with the new Roman governor, Festus, and agrees (26:32) that Paul is not guilty of any crime, and could have been set free had he not appealed to Caesar. Paul may still be a prisoner. But the gospel of the true Messiah has successfully confronted the rulers of the world.

Two other starting points. I said at the beginning that, with heaven and earth now joined in Jesus and the spirit, we shouldn't be surprised that most of the controversies in the book focus on temples. Well, the Temple is hardly mentioned in these closing chapters – though, in the Psalms, the Temple, like earth itself, is founded on the seas and prepared on the floods, and when they rage and swell God's city rises above them.[1] That's all in Luke's background here. But temples, anyway, being places where heaven and earth are joined, are thus places of *power*. In the first half of the book, the church confronts the Jerusalem authorities. Now Paul confronts the Roman governor and the man who at that time was known (though Luke doesn't call him this) as 'king of the Judeans', Herod Agrippa II. And with Agrippa, we run into questions we ourselves now face, as Western secularism increasingly tries to bully the Church to shut up and come into line.

So let's begin, as we did in the previous section, with a quick survey of these final four chapters.

Messianic thinking

We pick up the story in chapter 25. Paul has been under house arrest in Caesarea, while inept Felix can't figure out what to do with him, and the Judean authorities – and the mob! – still want him killed. Then Felix is replaced as governor by Porcius Festus; as was often the case with a change of ruler, Festus is eager to get through the administrative backlog and show the local hierarchy that he was someone they could trust and work with.

---

1   Psalm 24:1–2.

And then there's King Agrippa. His father, Herod Agrippa I, came to a bad end in Acts 12. Now the son, educated in Rome, sophisticated and cosmopolitan in outlook, has become officially 'king of the Judeans'. Like his forebears, he works hard for the well-being of Judean communities in both the homeland and the Diaspora. The Herod family, of course, lacked any actual royal, let alone messianic, credentials, so they were always eager to remind worldwide Judeans of their implicit claims. That's why, right up to the end, they were rebuilding and adorning the Temple, so that God might come back at last and dwell with his people, exalting them over the nations as he had always promised. (Remember how that symbol worked: David planned the Temple, Solomon built it, Hezekiah and Josiah cleansed it, Zerubbabel was supposed to rebuild it. Judas Maccabeus cleansed it – and even though he wasn't from the line of David, that was enough to set up him and his family as a new 'royal' house for a hundred years.) Thus, even though Herod Agrippa wasn't descended from David, there was still a sense that perhaps he might become, as it were, an honorary Davidic king, if he could do the business. Thus, behind all the (in other respects bizarre) royal claims of the house of Herod, we should detect the true hope of Israel: that one day the true Messiah would come, would rebuild the Temple for God to return at last, and would establish God's reign of justice and peace in the world.

Some of Agrippa's subjects did indeed wonder aloud whether he might be the true coming king of the Judeans, the Messiah. In particular, at home in the imperial world of Rome, but wanting to be a loyal Judean, Agrippa invested time and energy trying (and eventually failing) to keep the peace between Rome and the Judeans. So when Festus arrives, he needs to get to know Agrippa – and particularly to get his help with the tricky question of Paul.

Those of Luke's readers who understood how royal and messianic thinking worked in the first-century Judean world would realise the massive irony building up in these chapters. Paul is an emissary of the true Messiah, who is himself (along with his people) the true 'Temple'. The Messiah's people are already (from Paul's point of view) becoming the new community of justice and peace in the world. Now this Paul will at last meet Agrippa, the last best hope of the Judean monarchies of the period. Luke might almost be suggesting that, before Paul goes to Rome to confront the present ruler of the world, he must confront the present official king of the Judeans.

In both cases, Paul's witness will be not just to a different king, but to a different *kind* of king. Either way, it isn't simply the case that Herod Agrippa is the final person in Luke's story to hear Paul's tale. The fact is, more specifically, that Agrippa has been doing his best to symbolise the messianic hope of Israel: the hope which, in Paul's gospel, is of course fulfilled in Jesus himself.

All of that irony is bubbling along underneath chapter 25, including the famous twist in verses 1–11. Festus wants to do the Judeans a favour, so he suggests that Paul might stand trial in Jerusalem. Paul smells a plot. He knows that if he gets sent from Caesarea back to Jerusalem someone will probably be planning an ambush on the way. So, one more time, he tells the governor his business: this is the official tribunal, and that's where he ought to be tried. So he appeals to Caesar. Aha, the reader thinks: now at last we see how he's going to get to Rome.

But then (25:13–22) Festus wants Agrippa's help in figuring out what to write to Caesar. If he's sending a prisoner because he can't settle his case, the emperor will at least want to know what it's all about. As we see in verse 19, echoing once more the dismissive phrase of Gallio in 18:15, all Festus can hear is 'various wranglings concerning [the Judean] religion, and about some dead man called Jesus whom Paul asserted was alive'. That's a big puzzle for the governor. As elsewhere, you can't fit Jesus' resurrection into anyone else's world view. That isn't surprising; the resurrection inaugurates God's new creation. It transforms the old world, but it can't fit into the categories of the old world. It brings its own renewed world view with it.

Paul and the rulers of the world

So in verses 23–7 Festus invites Agrippa to come and hear Paul. That brings us, with a flourish of trumpets and drums, to chapter 26; here comes King Agrippa himself, with his sister Bernice beside him. Had there been a first-century equivalent of the UK's *Hello!* magazine (or, for the USA, *People* magazine), Bernice would seldom have been out of its pages. She is one of the first-century high-ranking women about whom we know quite a bit. She was, as we might say, quite a lady. Luke's readers would know exactly who she was.

So: this is Paul's chance to shine on the big stage. Jesus had said that his followers would stand before rulers and kings.[2] Isaiah, long ago, had prophesied that kings would shut their mouths before the Servant; that's part of the introduction to the fourth Servant Song, before the suffering of the Servant is portrayed and interpreted.[3] So then, in 26:2–23, Paul recapitulates and amplifies the Damascus Road story and its meaning one more time.

As in chapter 22, however, he doesn't get to the end of the story. In chapter 22, the mob rioted when he mentions the Gentiles. This time Festus the governor breaks in, curiously around the same point in the story, shouting that Paul is crazy. But Paul rounds it off with a cheeky in-your-face appeal to the supposedly loyal Judean Agrippa himself. Surely, Agrippa, you will admit that you believe the prophets, and that you believe in resurrection? Agrippa, wanting to position himself as the defender of all things Judean, can hardly deny that. But the chapter finishes in verses 30–2 with Festus and Agrippa agreeing that Paul had done nothing deserving even imprisonment, let alone more serious punishment.

But Paul has appealed to Caesar, and to Caesar he will go – but by way of a sea voyage at the wrong time of year, after the normal sailing season. If chapter 26 is one of Luke's great set-piece speeches, chapter 27 is his great artistic depiction of the storm and shipwreck. He paints it lavishly, like a huge canvas, with the ship in the middle, tossing and pitching, the crew and passengers holding on for dear life, and Paul on deck praying, telling people what to do, breaking bread . . . until they are all in the water and gasping and splashing

---

2 Mark 13:9.

3 Isaiah 52:13 – 53:12.

their way to shore. This is not just a vivid piece of writing, a kind of verbal film for an excited first-century audience. It is that, to be sure, but there's much more, as we shall see in a moment.

Chapter 28 is a kind of long-drawn-out sigh of relief. It ends with what looks like a question mark; but (as I said before) the point of Luke's story is not what happened to Paul, but what happened to the gospel. So we have a couple of quick scenes on Malta: verses 1–6 with the bonfire (and the snake that might have killed Paul, but which in fact does him no harm) and verses 7–10 with Paul exercising a healing ministry. Then (verses 11–16) it's off to Rome at last. But before Paul faces Nero, he has other important business, as we might have guessed from the letter to the Romans itself. What about the Judean community there?

The background is important. Rome in this period had around a million inhabitants, counting both slaves and free people. Within that, the Jewish community numbered in the thousands, possibly even ten or twenty thousand, having returned in AD 54 after their earlier expulsion under Claudius. The Christians in Rome, meanwhile, numbered at the most perhaps two hundred. That's a rough guess, but it comports with the different house-churches addressed by Paul in Romans 16. They seemed to have been divided into a few little groups, crammed most likely into somebody's attic, or the room behind a shop, living quite probably in the poorer parts of town, not least in Trastevere, across the River Tiber from where Nero was building his vast and opulent palace, the Domus Aurea ('Golden House'). Despite their tiny numbers, the Christian groups in Rome were already seen by the larger population as dangerous subversives. Anyone meeting together in private in groups that didn't match the normal social expectations was obviously up to no good.

But the little Christian communities were not the big worry for Paul. The real problem was in the Judean communities. Judeans, in their well-established communities around the Mediterranean and beyond, were well aware that things back home in the Middle East were reaching boiling point. Rome kept sending inept or provocative governors to try to keep the lid on an increasingly volatile situation, but many of them simply made matters worse. So what would happen to the Judeans in Rome if Rome went to war against the Judeans in Galilee and Judea? Claudius had kicked the Judeans out of Rome because of riots, due (according to the historian Suetonius) to someone called *Chrestus*. A good many historians think this is a garbled reference to the gospel of Jesus '*Christos*' arriving among the Judean inhabitants in Rome, with results that we could predict from seeing what happened in the cities Paul had visited. Would Nero do the same again, expelling the Judeans from Rome, if he suspected them of supporting the cause of their relatives in their ancient homeland? And – some Judeans in Rome might wonder – had *Paul come here to tell the emperor he had better do just that*? That is the context for Paul's gospel exposition to them in 28:17–29.

In the shadows here, unstated like a character in a Beckett play, was Nero himself. Now as all through, Paul, a good creational monotheist, believes that God has placed human authorities in power. But the balancing truth is that it's the church's task to hold them to account when they fail to do their job.[4] How was that going to work out? Luke leaves us to wonder.

Four great themes

There, then, are the final four chapters of Acts. I see four great themes here, reaching a fitting though tantalising conclusion, and pointing us ahead in our own mission and life.

First, and always central, there is the world-changing message of Jesus' resurrection. Festus's summary in 25:19 is touchingly naive: a muddle of wranglings concerning the Jewish religion, and a rumour about some dead chap whom Paul said was alive! Luke's readers know what this is about, though it does feel odd, suddenly, to see it through the eyes of an uncomprehending pagan. The point, though, is obvious: through Jesus' resurrection, a new world order

---

4   See my *JP* (with Michael F. Bird), esp. ch. 3.

has been unveiled, declaring him to be both king of the Judeans and lord of the world. Luke is showing how this is now being announced to Agrippa, the present king of the Jews, the friend of Caesar who is the present official lord of the world. So the book concludes with Paul speaking of God as king and Jesus as lord 'with no one stopping him' (28:31) – quite something, when we consider how many people had been trying to stop him for most of the previous fifteen chapters. Paul, whether legally or not, was claiming and exercising in Rome the freedom of speech and assembly that had been granted in Corinth, but which was hotly contested in many other places.

Paul's summary statement before Agrippa emphasises the radical change in the people of God. Acts 26:18 seems to me to have particular force: Paul's commission was to be sent to the nations,

> so that you can open their eyes to enable them to turn from darkness to light, and from the power of the satan to God – so that they can have forgiveness of sins, and an inheritance among those who are made holy, by their faith in me.

Paul's mission to the Gentiles was aimed, not at creating a Gentile church in parallel to a Judean one, but at *incorporating Gentiles into God's ancient people.*

Let's be clear once more. The Judean objection to pagans, and the reason for the different taboos (variously interpreted but always there) against fraternising too closely with them, was that they were idolaters and thus automatically sinners and unclean, in the grip of the satan, the accuser. Paul's answer was not a new regime of 'tolerance' in which sin and all that stuff didn't matter any more. Paul's answer was that *the gospel provided the remedy.* As Paul says in Colossians 1:12–14, the gospel delivers people from the power of darkness and transfers them into the kingdom of God's beloved son, 'in whom we have redemption, the forgiveness of sins'.

Echoing this, Paul here insists, in Acts 26:18, that the gospel will open the eyes of the Gentiles, turning them from darkness to light, and from the satan's power to God's power, so that by faith in Jesus they may receive the double blessing – forgiveness of sins, and an inheritance among the sanctified. They will be, in other words, part of the true people of God. *This is justification by faith*: not so much an individual transaction, aimed at escaping the world and going to heaven, but the declaration that all believers, whatever their ethnic, cultural or religious background, are forgiven and sanctified, and hence part of the single renewed family of God – all because they belong to the crucified and risen Messiah. So what is required of Gentiles, as in 26:20, is that they should repent of idolatry, turn to the true God, and do the works that follow. If this sounds familiar, it may be because it reflects Pauline summaries such as that in 1 Thessalonians 1:9–10 and elsewhere.

So, yet again, Paul has turned the tables. Faced with an uncomprehending Roman governor, he hasn't defended himself against the charges of being anti-torah, anti-Temple or anti-Caesar. He has gone behind all those, to the glorious unveiling of Jesus. Jesus and his gospel provide a deeper reality than torah to define and direct God's people; they bring about a fresh joining of heaven and earth which would upstage the Temple once and for all; and they reveal the world's true lord, 'another king', who would offer an oblique though powerful challenge to Caesar. Luke's reader will get all that, even if poor old Festus got a headache. And we are left wondering whether Agrippa's line in verse 28 was quizzical or merely sarcastic ('You reckon you're going to make *me* a Christian, then, and pretty quick, too, by the sound of it!'). Ultimately, Paul's defence is to restate the gospel message, and let it do its own work.

My first theme, then, has been the message of Jesus' resurrection and its implications. The second theme, growing out of this, is the way Paul was trying to work for large-scale reconciliation. Paul, I suggest, was in his way doing the same thing as King Agrippa was trying to do – but with Jesus in the middle of it. I suspect that Luke knows this very well and is using the scene with Agrippa to make the point.

Agrippa, you see, was trying to negotiate peace and mutual tolerance between imperial Rome and loyal Judaism. He was hoping on the one hand to get Rome to govern more sensitively. He and his sister Bernice were hoping on the other hand to get Judean revolutionaries to calm down and accept Roman rule, and learn to practise their torah-obedience within that framework.

Paul was steering a similar but different course. He was fiercely loyal to the heritage of Israel, albeit as redefined around Jesus as Messiah. He was cheerfully using his Roman citizenship to get him out of trouble and safely to Rome. Agrippa was trying to persuade Roman officials to behave better; Paul, believing that the authorities had a God-given job, would regularly remind them what that job entailed. Agrippa was hoping to get the Judeans to back off from violent revolt; Paul was praying that they would accept Jesus as the prince of peace. As we today face huge questions about faith and policy – different questions in different parts of the world, but all going on together – we need to abandon the sterile eighteenth-century antithesis of being either 'for' or 'against' our rulers, and find fresh ways to demonstrate in action what it means that Jesus is lord of the whole world.

Luke can help us with that task. We need to think through from scratch the ways in which Paul's teaching elsewhere about the 'principalities and powers' grows out of these challenges in the first century and enables us to address the equivalent challenges in our own day. As I've said before, it's noticeable that in Ephesians, where Paul most obviously celebrates Jesus' victory over the powers, and the fact that his people share in that victory and in Jesus' worldwide rule, the letter ends with a sober and serious warning about spiritual warfare. If we ponder what Luke is doing in these splendid scenes, we may begin to see paths through our difficulties, and be able to notice and develop every fresh chance of working for reconciliation and for God's kingdom.

If we even make a start with this, we will face the third great theme of these closing chapters. Luke has structured the Gospel and Acts in parallel. Jesus' long journey to Jerusalem in Luke 9 – 19 ends with his crucifixion: 'Your moment has come at last,' he says, 'and so has the power of darkness' (22:53). Paul's long journey of chapters 13 – 21 reaches its climax with the storm and the shipwreck. Put the two side by side: Acts 27 matches Luke 22 – 23.

The power of darkness does its worst. *This is what you can expect if you set off on the gospel journey.*

The voyage and shipwreck have echoes across ancient literature, especially Homer's *Odyssey*. Odysseus, one of the great heroes of the Trojan War, has a long sea voyage before he can get back to his home in Ithaca. Many dangers and trials stand in his way, and some at least of Luke's readers might well have thought of Odysseus as they read Luke's story of Paul. But Luke's hero Paul, though he's similar in some ways, isn't going home. He is on God's business, going metaphorically to the ends of the earth.

But the really important background is the biblical one. In Genesis 1:2, God's spirit, his great wind, broods over the dark waters to produce creation. Noah and his family – and his floating zoo – are rescued from the flood which comes to destroy the world. The exodus focuses on Moses leading the people through the sea and on towards their promised inheritance. The Psalms speak of the mighty waters raging and roaring, and God overcoming the dark waters, and rescuing his people. Jonah sails west to escape God's call, and the sailors throw him overboard because he's bringing them bad luck; but Paul sails west to obey God's call, and he stands tall in the boat and tells everyone not to panic and certainly not to abandon ship prematurely. And perhaps above all, in Daniel 7 the monsters come up out of the sea, and God exalts the One like a son of man and installs him as lord of the world. If you're going to tell the story of the gospel confronting the powers of the world, Daniel 7 is the passage to evoke, bringing with it all those other echoes as well. Acts 27 does just that. Here comes Paul to establish the new western base of missionary operations. Is it any wonder that the dark powers try to stop him?

The others on the boat might easily have seen Paul as the problem: like Jonah, it's his fault all this is happening! I suspect Paul's own friends sometimes thought, 'If only he hadn't appealed to Caesar, we might have had a much easier journey.' But this is how it often is. As you launch out in faith, in ministry, in new ventures, don't be surprised if the winds suddenly blow you apparently off course, and you find yourself drifting towards the rocks. It happens.

It doesn't mean you've done the wrong thing or failed in your loyalty. Of course, you *may* have done; that is always a distinct possibility; and you should be humbly aware of that risk and discuss it frankly with a wise spiritual guide. But it's just as likely that you really are breaking ground for the gospel, and that the dark powers are trying to resist.

That happened, of course, when Jesus began his public career. As soon as he started announcing in the synagogues that it was time for God to become king, then (as we might say) all hell broke loose. Opposition of all sorts came out of the woodwork. I have seen that again and again, both when people are training for ministry and when they start a new phase of their vocation. By placing this wonderful story in parallel to the crucifixion scene, Luke has said: the gospel message of God's victory over the dark powers on the cross must now be *implemented* by the same means – by the followers of Jesus bearing the cross, facing the darkness and the sea-monsters. And it's in that context that Paul takes charge: 'If these men don't stay in the ship, there is no chance of safety' (27:31). Luke may be saying that to people he knows in some churches, tempted to leave in search of easier options. But the challenge is always there. When we read New Testament books such as 1 Peter or Revelation, we see it plainly. The suffering of Jesus' followers is the means by which the victory won on the cross is to be implemented in the world.

The way Luke has told the story, again, picks up from the parallel with the crucifixion scene: this is the way of *salvation*. There's a sudden rush of 'salvation' language in chapter 27 (which doesn't always appear in modern translations such as my own). To read the passage literally, we find Luke saying in verse 20 that all hope of being *saved* was lost; then in verse 31 Paul declares that if these men don't stay on board, there's no chance of being *saved*; in verse 34 he urges them to 'take some bread for your *salvation*' (Luke surely wants this to resonate as a eucharistic hint in the middle of the storm). Then, in verses 43 and 44, the centurion wanted (literally) to *save* Paul, and they all ended up *thoroughly saved, diasōthēnai*, on the land. Luke rubs it in in 28:1 and 4, where, again literally, they've been 'thoroughly saved' and then where Paul is 'saved' from the snake.

As with the cross itself, God works his saving purposes for, and through, those who cling to him in the dark and stormy sea.

Remember, then: 'salvation' for Luke clearly means, as it did for Paul, the Creator God calling his whole creation to order, overcoming and destroying all the powers that corrupt and enslave his beautiful creation. More especially will he rescue his image-bearing human creatures, bringing forth by his spirit the new world, the ultimate heaven-plus-earth world, in which the royal priesthood will be the image-bearing humans who have been raised from the dead, 'saved' from the corruption and death that are the result of idolatry and sin.

So the salvation Luke is describing is, as we might say, 'this-worldly'. It anticipates, and draws its meaning from, the ultimate 'salvation' which is not *from* the world but *of* and *for* the world.

So: we have, first, the world-changing message of the resurrection; second, the political navigation between earthly power and the people of God; third, the battle with the sea-monster, the dark power that opposes God's rescuing purposes and the people who are carrying them out. Fourth and finally, we have the innocence not only of Paul but of the gospel itself.

Think back to Philippi, Athens, Corinth and Ephesus: in each place, the authorities had to admit that Paul was in the clear. In Corinth, Gallio gave his judgement that the gospel itself was legally permitted; the praxis and message of the Jesus-followers was to be allowed *as a valid form of the Judean way of life*. Now, in these closing chapters, we have seen that, in Caesarea, the Roman governor and the king of the Judeans agree: Paul has done nothing wrong. They comment that he could have been released, had he not gone and appealed to Caesar. Once again we note the parallel, of which Luke is fully aware in constructing his Gospel and Acts. In the Gospel, Jesus is repeatedly found innocent, but he dies the death of the guilty. In Acts, Paul is repeatedly found innocent, but he has to go through shipwreck to fulfil his commission, to bring the message to Rome openly and unhindered.

In particular, in 28:17–28, he has to explain to the Judean leaders in Rome that he hasn't come to stir up trouble for them. This may seem like a side issue to us, but (as I hinted a moment ago) it was anything but. In his letter to the Roman church, Paul had urged his Gentile readers not to look down on the unbelieving Judeans, not to imagine that God had cut them off for ever. Paul had declared that, as apostle to the Gentiles, he made much of his ministry precisely in order that he might make his fellow Judeans 'jealous' *and so save some of them*. He wasn't expecting a large-scale last-minute conversion of all or most of them. But he was expecting, praying for and working for a good relationship between the scattered and disorganised little churches and the much larger and more powerful and socially influential synagogue community, in the hope that the Judean inhabitants of Rome might come to see that the Jesus whom these small groups were worshipping really was Israel's Messiah. Just as Paul had gone to Jerusalem with hopes of being able to persuade many Judean residents and pilgrims of the truth of the gospel, so I think he came to Rome with the same positive intent. This is where we see him trying to put it into effect. Once more, he tries to explain to learned Judeans how the gospel of Messiah Jesus is indeed the fulfilment of Scripture. One more time, some believe but others don't.

But the other thing he is concerned about is of course that the Judeans in Rome, very much aware of the situation in Judea and Galilee, might wonder if Paul had come to stir up trouble. Perhaps, they may have thought, he was about to tell the imperial authorities that the unbelieving Judeans back in their homeland were causing problems that Rome had better address in the usual way.

It seems that the Judean leaders in Rome were able to put Paul's mind at rest on this score. They hadn't had any messages about him. All they knew was that everywhere the new sect was spoken against. However, reading between the lines, we hear nothing of the synagogue communities trying to persuade the Roman officials to persecute the Christians. Persecution will happen soon enough, because very soon Nero will single them out as scapegoats for the great fire. But before that, the gospel will be announced and taught openly and unhindered. It will take root and grow.

Last time I was in Rome, we were taken to a newly discovered archaeological site, beside the Corso, the main north–south road in the middle of town. There's a room in a basement under the

Doria Pamphilj gallery, now below street level, where the researchers have found wall paintings which indicate that it was seen very early on as a specially holy place. They reckon that's where Paul was kept in imprisonment. It is moving beyond words to sit there and ponder Paul's imprisonment.

It is also striking to take the short walk up the street from there to a tall second-century column. This column originally had a statue of the emperor Marcus Aurelius on top. On top now is a statue of Paul himself. Openly and unhindered. As various people have pointed out in our own day, reflecting on Paul's hearing before the emperor, the time would come when people would name their dogs 'Nero' and their sons 'Paul'.

But Paul's trial – which is kept off stage by Luke, either because it hadn't happened yet or because he didn't want to distract from the main message – makes its own theological point. Luke has repeatedly recorded the verdicts of 'innocent', 'not guilty', 'done nothing wrong' against Paul, all looking ahead to the moment off stage when he will hear Caesar's final verdict. Luke is telling us already, in advance, in the present time, what the final verdict will be.

Do you see the point? *That is exactly how Paul's doctrine of justification works.* In Romans 2, Paul insists that there will be a final judgement, yet to come. But in Romans 3, he explains that the Messiah's people, with Jesus-shaped faith as their badge, have already heard the verdict. It has been announced in advance. The verdict 'in the right' has been brought forward from the future into the present. Already we know that 'there is now no condemnation for those in the Messiah, Jesus' (Romans 8:1). The verdict has been declared, even before the final trial has taken place.

Scholars have often debated whether Luke gets Paul's theology right. Here he has not only got it right; he has woven it into his narrative. Whatever storms and shipwrecks may come, Jesus' followers already know the final verdict. When God raised Jesus from the dead, he not only declared that Jesus was indeed his son, the Messiah and lord. He declared that all Jesus' people share that sonship, already now and in the age to come when we too will be raised to share his new creation. And in the present time we, like Paul, are charged and tasked with announcing God as king and Jesus as lord.

Conclusion

By no means all Jesus' followers today are able to announce Jesus as lord 'openly and unhindered', as Paul was in Rome. We should pray for those who have to do it secretly and under duress. But as long as we in the Western churches are able to, we shouldn't mess around. The resurrection of Jesus is not only the central datum of our faith. It is the source of the energy we need, which we must claim for our task. We too face the challenges of the dark forces that seek to prevent us getting where our calling is pointing, and doing what we believe we should. Like Paul in the boat, we must hang on and be prayerful and patient. And we need to hear again and again the gospel verdict, already in the present, anticipating the time when our own resurrection will be God's way of saying, 'There: I told you all along you were my beloved children.' As we thank God for Luke and his remarkable work, we thank God that Luke's story of the gospel, getting to the ends of the earth, is our story as well. And we pray for grace and strength to live and proclaim it with all boldness, and with no one stopping us.

Suggestions for Further Reading

There are many fine works on Acts; this is a small selection of recent books. At the scholarly level, Barrett, Keener, Schnabel and Walton provide a wealth of discussion and a full range of secondary literature. At the popular level, Alexander (2006), Gaventa, Jennings and Wright (2008) offer suggestive application. Many issues in Acts are taken up in books about Paul and the early church, a good example being Winter (2001); reading Acts thoughtfully also requires a working knowledge of the history of the first-century church in its social and cultural contexts, on which there is of course a vast range of material, summarised at a popular level in my *The New Testament in Its World* (*NTW*) (with Michael F. Bird).

Recent books on Acts, mainly commentaries, include the following:

Alexander, Loveday (2005), *Acts in Its Ancient Literary Context: A classicist looks at the Acts of the Apostles*, London: Bloomsbury.

Alexander, Loveday (2006), *Acts: The people's Bible commentary*, Oxford: Bible Reading Fellowship. (Loveday Alexander is also preparing a fresh commentary on Acts in the Black's New Testament Commentary series.)

Barrett, C. K. (1994, 1998), *The Acts of the Apostles*, International Critical Commentary, 2 vols, Edinburgh and London: T&T Clark.

Gaventa, B. R. (2003), *Acts*, Abingdon New Testament Commentaries, Nashville, TN: Abingdon.

Jennings, Willie James (2017), *Acts*, Belief: A Theological Commentary on the Bible, Louisville, KY: Westminster John Knox.

Keener, Craig (2020), *Acts*, New Cambridge Bible Commentary, Cambridge: Cambridge University Press. This is a masterly abbreviation of Keener's massive four-volume commentary, published by Baker Book House in Grand Rapids, MI, 2012–15.

Schnabel, E. J. (2012), *Acts*, Zondervan Exegetical Commentary on the New Testament, Grand Rapids, MI: Zondervan.

Walton, Steve (2024), *Acts 1–9*, Word Biblical Commentaries, Grand Rapids, MI: Zondervan. Further volumes in preparation.

Walton, Steve (2024), *Reading Acts Theologically*, London: T&T Clark.

Winter, Bruce W. (2001), *After Paul Left Corinth: The influence of secular ethics and social change*, Grand Rapids, MI: Eerdmans.

Witherington, Ben (1998), *The Acts of the Apostles: A socio-rhetorical commentary*, Grand Rapids, MI: Eerdmans.

Wright, Tom (2008), *Acts for Everyone*, 2 vols, London: SPCK; Louisville, KY: Westminster John Knox.

Among my own previous works I have cited the following:

2003	*For All the Saints? Remembering the Christian departed* (*FAS*), London: SPCK.
2003	*The Resurrection of the Son of God* (*RSG*), Christian Origins and the Question of God 3, London: SPCK; Minneapolis, MN: Fortress.
2004	(with Michael F. Bird), *Jesus and the Powers: Christian political witness in an age of totalitarian terror and dysfunctional democracies* (*JP*), London: SPCK; Grand Rapids, MI: Zondervan.
2007, 2008	*Surprised by Hope* (*SH*), London: SPCK; San Francisco, CA: HarperOne.
2013	*Paul and the Faithfulness of God* (*PFG*), Christian Origins and the Question of God 4, London: SPCK; Minneapolis, MN: Fortress.
2015	*Paul and His Recent Interpreters* (*PRI*), London: SPCK; Minneapolis, MN: Fortress.
2018	*Paul: A Biography* (*PB*), London: SPCK; San Francisco, CA: HarperOne.

2019   *History and Eschatology: Jesus and the promise
         of natural theology* (*HE*), Gifford Lectures 2018,
         London: SPCK; Waco, TX: Baylor University Press.

2019   · (with Michael F. Bird), *The New Testament in Its
         World: An introduction to the history, literature and
         theology of the first Christians* (*NTW*), London:
         SPCK; Grand Rapids, MI: Zondervan.

2020   *Broken Signposts: How the gospel makes sense of
         the world* (*BS*), London: SPCK; San Francisco, CA:
         HarperOne.

2021   *Galatians*, Christian Formation Commentaries,
         Grand Rapids, MI: Eerdmans.

Index

Index

Index

Index

Into the Heart of Romans

A Deep Dive into Paul's Greatest Letter

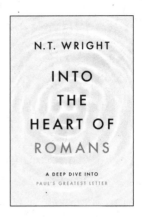

Romans is often and for good reason considered a crux of Christian thought and theology, the greatest of Paul's letters. And within Romans, chapter 8 is one of the most spectacular pieces of early Christian writing.

Yet to many readers, Romans can be a deceptively difficult book. Its scope and basic meaning may be clear, but it can be hard to see how it all fits together into a cohesive, if complex, doctrinal argument.

N. T. Wright—widely regarded as one of the most influential commentators and interpreters of Paul today—deftly unpacks this dense and sometimes elusive letter, detailing Paul's arguments and showing how it illuminates the gospel from the promises to Abraham through the visions of Revelation. Wright takes a deep dive into Romans 8, showing how it illuminates so much else that God reveals in Scripture: God the Father, Christology, and the Spirit; Jesus' messiahship, cross, resurrection, and ascension; salvation, redemption, and adoption; suffering and glory; holiness and hope.

Into the Heart of Romans will help you become familiar with the book of Romans in a deeper way that will also deepen your understanding and appreciation of the gospel itself.

The New Testament in Its World

An Introduction to the History, Literature, and Theology of the First Christians

N. T. Wright and Michael F. Bird

This volume is a readable, one-volume introduction placing the entire New Testament and early Christianity in its original context. An ideal guide for students, *The New Testament in Its World* addresses the many difficult questions faced by those studying early Christianity, including:

- What was the first-century understanding of the kingdom of God?
- What is the meaning of the resurrection in its original context?
- What were the Gospels, and how did they come about?
- Who was Paul and why are his letters so controversial?

Written for both classroom and personal use, this book brings together decades of ground-breaking research, writing, and teaching into one volume. It presents the New Testament books—along with their subjects: Jesus and the early church—within the historical and social context of Second Temple Judaism and Greco-Roman politics and culture.

The New Testament in Its World allows you to recover the excitement of what it was like to live as Christians in the first or second centuries.

Also available are video and workbook companion resources (sold separately) to enhance learning and experience the world of the New Testament.

Available in stores and online!

ZONDERVAN®
.com